JONES & BARTLETT LEARNING INFORMATION SYSTEMS SECURITY & ASSURANCE SERIES

LABORATORY MANUAL TO ACCOMPANY

Hacker Techniques, Tools, and Incident Handling

VERSION 1.5

virtualsecurity CLOUD labs powered by TOOLWIRE

VLAB SOLUTIONS

JONES & BARTLETT LEARNING

World Headquarters
Jones & Bartlett Learning
5 Wall Street
Burlington, MA 01803
978-443-5000
info@jblearning.com
www.jblearning.com

Jones & Bartlett Learning books and products are available through most bookstores and online booksellers. To contact Jones & Bartlett Learning directly, call 800-832-0034, fax 978-443-8000, or visit our website, www.jblearning.com.

Substantial discounts on bulk quantities of Jones & Bartlett Learning publications are available to corporations, professional associations, and other qualified organizations. For details and specific discount information, contact the special sales department at Jones & Bartlett Learning via the above contact information or send an email to specialsales@jblearning.com.

Production Credits
Chief Executive Officer: Ty Field
President: James Homer
SVP, Editor-in-Chief: Michael Johnson
SVP, Chief Marketing Officer: Alison M. Pendergast
SVP, Curriculum Solutions: Christopher Will
Director of Sales, Curriculum Solutions: Randi Roger
Author: vLab Solutions, LLC, David Kim, President
Editorial Management: High Stakes Writing, LLC, Lawrence J. Goodrich, Editor and Publisher
Copy Editor, High Stakes Writing: Katherine Dillin
Copy Editor, High Stakes Writing: Ruth Walker
Senior Editorial Assistant: Rainna Erikson
Reprints and Special Projects Manager: Susan Schultz
Associate Production Editor: Tina Chen
Rights & Photo Research Associate: Lian Bruno
Manufacturing and Inventory Control Supervisor: Amy Bacus
Senior Marketing Manager: Andrea DeFronzo
Cover Design: Anne Spencer
Composition: CAE Solutions Corp.
Cover Image: © Handy Widiyanto/ShutterStock, Inc.
Printing and Binding: Edwards Brothers Malloy
Cover Printing: Edwards Brothers Malloy

ISBN: 978-1-284-03754-8

6048
Printed in the United States of America
17 16 15 14 13 10 9 8 7 6 5 4 3 2 1

Contents

Ethics and Code of Conduct

The material presented in this course is designed to give you a real-life look at the use of various tools and systems that are at the heart of every network security analyst's daily responsibilities. Through use of this material, you will have access to software and techniques used every day by professionals. With this access come certain ethical responsibilities.

The hardware, software, tools, and applications presented and used in this lab manual and/or the VSCL are intended to be used for instructional and educational purposes only.

As a student in this course, you are not to use these tools, applications, or techniques on live production IT infrastructures inside or outside of your campus or organization. Under no circumstances are you permitted to use these tools, applications, or techniques on the production IT infrastructures and networks of other organizations.

You are required to conform to your school or organization's Code of Conduct and ethics policies during the use of this lab manual and any of the tools, applications, or techniques described within.

Preface

Welcome! This lab manual is your step-by-step guide to completing the laboratory exercises for this course.

Virtual Security Cloud Lab (VSCL)

For most of the exercises in this lab manual, you will use the Virtual Security Cloud Lab (VSCL) resource.

> **Note:**
> The Virtual Security Cloud Lab requires use of either **Windows Internet Explorer** or **Mozilla Firefox**. The Virtual Security Cloud Lab does not support Google Chrome, Safari, or Opera at this time.

The VSCL is a collection of virtual resources, including Windows and Linux servers, Cisco routers, and applications such as Wireshark, FileZilla, and Nessus®, that will allow you to perform all of the tasks in this lab manual as if you were performing them in a live production environment. The heart of the VSCL is a Windows Workstation desktop configured to give you access to the tools and resources you need for each lab, without any special setup on your part.

As noted in the following table, some of the exercises in this lab manual will be performed without using the VSCL. For detailed instructions on how to perform these exercises, please consult your syllabus or instructor.

How to Use This Lab Manual

This lab manual features step-by-step instructions for completing the following hands-on lab exercises:

VSCL	LAB TITLE
No	Lab #1: Develop an Attack and Penetration Test Plan
Yes	Lab #2: Implement Hashing and Encryption for Secure Communications
No	Lab #3: Perform Data Gathering and Footprinting on a Targeted Website
Yes	Lab #4: Compromise and Exploit a Vulnerable Microsoft® Workstation
Yes	Lab #5: Perform a Website and Database Attack by Exploiting Identified Vulnerabilities
Yes	Lab #6: Identify and Mitigate Malware and Malicious Software on a Windows Server
Yes	Lab #7: Conduct a Network Traffic Analysis and Baseline Definition
Yes	Lab #8: Audit and Implement a Secure WLAN Solution
Yes	Lab #9: Perform Incident Response for an Infected Microsoft® Windows Workstation
Yes	Lab #10: Design and Implement SNORT as an Intrusion Detection System (IDS)

Video Walkthroughs of Each Lab

Each VSCL-based exercise in this lab manual includes a video walkthrough that gives you a quick overview of every step and function. You can watch the video walkthrough prior to performing the lab exercise, and refer to it as necessary while you complete the lab. You can pause, rewind, and fast-forward the video walkthroughs if you need to take notes or spend extra time on a particular step or function. Consult your syllabus or instructor for information on where to locate the walkthrough videos.

Step-by-Step Instructions

You'll find it easy to complete these lab exercises by following the detailed step-by-step instructions. Each step is clearly broken down into sub-steps, and all actions you are required to take are noted in **bold** font. Screenshots are included to help you identify key menus, dialog boxes, and input locations. If you get stuck on a step, refer to the lab video, which follows the order of the steps.

Deliverables

At the completion of each lab, you'll be asked to provide a set of deliverables to your instructor. These deliverables may include documents, files, screenshots, and/or answers to assessment questions. The deliverables are designed to test your understanding of the information, and your successful completion of the steps and functions of the lab. For specific information on deliverables, refer to the **Deliverables** section at the end of each lab.

> **Note:**
> Some labs require the use of a word processor such as Microsoft® Word for preparing and submitting deliverables. If you do not have access to a word processor, you can use OpenOffice on the Workstation desktop of the VSCL to prepare your documents. It includes a word processor called Writer that has all the features necessary for creating documents for use in these labs.

File Transfer

At times, you may be asked to transfer to another computer files you have created while performing lab steps in the VSCL. This can be performed using the File Transfer function built in to the vWorkstation desktop of the VSCL. Instructions for preparing and sending files using the File Transfer function can be found at the beginning of the video walkthrough for the first lab in each course (in most cases, Lab #1).

> **Note:**
> Use of this lab manual or the VSCL **does not require use of the textbook**. If you have questions about whether a textbook is needed for your course, consult your instructor.

Develop an Attack and Penetration Test Plan

LAB 1

Introduction

In this lab, you will follow a scenario in which you have been hired as an information systems security consultant. Your client has requested a written proposal for performing a penetration test on the company's production e-commerce Web application server and the CISCO core backbone network diagramed in Figure 1.1. As part of this scenario, you will research samples of existing penetration testing methodology and then use that research to create an attack and penetration test plan with a predefined table of contents.

This lab is a paper-based design lab and does not require use of the Virtual Security Cloud Lab (VSCL). To successfully complete the deliverables for this lab, you will need access to a text editor or word processor, such as Microsoft® Word. For some labs, you may also need access to a graphics line drawing application, such as Visio or PowerPoint.

> **Note:**
> If you don't have a word processor or graphics package, use OpenOffice on the student landing vWorkstation for your lab deliverables and to answer the lab assessment questions. To capture screenshots, **press Prt Sc > MSPAINT, paste** into a text document, and **save** the document in the Security_Strategies folder (**C:\Security_Strategies**) using the File Transfer function.

Learning Objectives and Outcomes

Upon completing this lab, you will be able to:

- Define the scope and requirements for the attack and penetration test plan
- Document the attack and penetration test plan scope, the major steps, the required data needed, and the expected data to be collected during the penetration test
- Analyze a targeted organization's profile and gather the preliminary reconnaissance information
- Design an attack and penetration test plan specific to gaining access to this organization's network
- Document an attack and penetration test plan on the targeted organization's network

Deliverables

Upon completion of this lab, you are required to provide the following deliverables to your instructor:

1. A written attack and penetration test plan for the scenario described in this lab;
2. Lab Assessment Questions & Answers for Lab #1.

Hands-On Steps

1. This lab begins with a formal request from John Smith, CEO of E-commerce Sales, a client of your information systems security consulting company. The client is requesting that you submit a proposal for performing a penetration test on the company's production e-commerce Web application server and its Cisco network (Figure 1.1) and has defined the parameters for the test in the table following.

   As the consultant assigned to this client, you will submit a proposed attack and penetration test plan describing your firm's approach to performing the penetration test and what specific tasks, deliverables, and reports you will complete as part of your services.

CLIENT PENETRATION TEST REQUEST	
Scope	Production e-commerce Web application server and Cisco network described in Figure 1.1. Located on ASA_Instructor, the e-commerce Web application server is acting as an external point-of-entry into the network: • Ubuntu Linux 10.04 LTS Server (TargetUbuntu01) • Apache Web Server running the e-commerce Web application server • Credit card transaction processing occurs
Intrusive or Non-Intrusive	Intrusive. The test will include penetrating past specific security checkpoints.
Compromise or No Compromise	No compromise. The test can compromise with written client authorization only.
Scheduling	Between 2:00 a.m.–6:00 a.m. EST weekend only (Saturday and Sunday)

FIGURE 1.1

Client's Cisco network

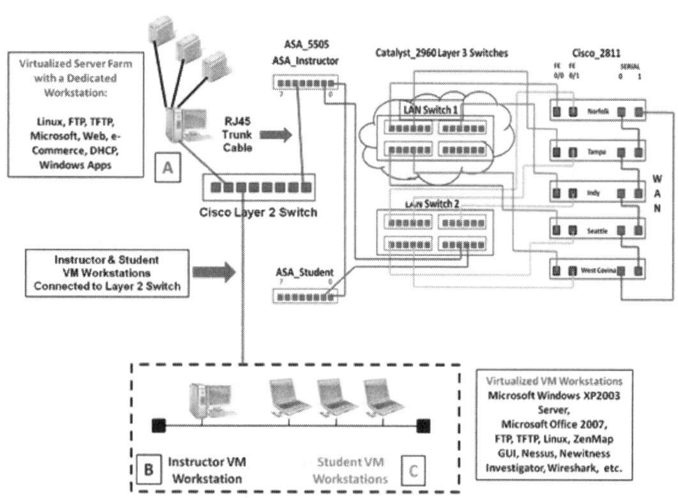

a. Five remote sites connect with one corporate headquarters.
b. WAN cloud provides connectivity to all sites.
c. WAN-to-LAN infrastructure consists of redundant trunk connections.
d. LAN infrastructure utilizes VLANs.
e. A Web-based e-commerce application server is located on ASA_Instructor acting as a DMZ or external point-of-entry into the network (i.e., Internet ingress/egress is on ASA_Instructor). Credit card transaction processing is taking place.
f. Remote sales representatives connect to HQ through a VPN tunnel to the ASA_Student. The ASA_Student provides secure remote access via VPN tunnels through the Internet.

> **Note:**
> The next steps will guide you through the steps you will take to create an attack and penetration test plan that meets your client's needs.

2. In a new text document, **create** an **Attack and Penetration Test Plan** that includes each of the following headings:
   - Table of Contents
   - Scope
   - Goals and Objectives
   - Tasks
   - Reporting
   - Schedule
   - Unanswered Questions
   - Authorization Letter

   You will follow the steps in this lab to complete the test plan as if you were an actual consultant for this client. You will be responsible for determining what to document and which actions fall into the headings established in your text document.
3. **Review** the **Hacking_Lab #1 Penetration Testing White Paper.pdf** handout for this lab. The document suggests a methodology for conducting a penetration test within an organization.

   If not available from your instructor, **use** the **File Transfer button** on the vWorkstation virtual machine to download this file from the Security_Strategies folder (**C:\Security_Strategies\Hacking\Hacking_Lab #1 Penetration Testing White Paper.pdf**).
4. From a workstation with Internet capability, **research** the following topics related to penetration testing. You will use this information to complete the deliverables for this lab:
   - Penetration testing methodology
   - Penetration test plans
   - NIST penetration testing documentation
   - Web application penetration testing
   - E-commerce penetration testing
   - Network penetration testing
   - Common tools and applications for penetration testing
   - Black box testing, grey box testing, Black/grey box testing
   - Social engineering testing
5. In your text document, **draft** a **Scope section** that defines what is within the scope of testing and what is out of scope. Explain what you can and cannot do as part of the test and justifications for each.
6. In your text document, **draft** a **Goals and Objectives section** that defines the rubrics for determining the success or failure of the testing.
7. In your text document, **draft** a **Tasks section** that defines the actual steps that a penetration tester will perform.
8. In your text document, **draft** a **Reporting section** that defines how the results of the tasks will be recorded, and by whom.
9. In your text document, **draft** a **Schedule section** that defines the dates and times for the testing to occur.
10. In your text document, **draft** an **Unanswered Questions section** that defines a list of requirements and preliminary questions you may have for the client before you can proceed with testing.
11. In your text document, **draft** an **Authorization Letter section** that will permit you to perform a penetration test on the client's production environment without liability.
12. **Submit** the **text document** to your instructor as a deliverable for this lab.

Evaluation Criteria and Rubrics

The following are the evaluation criteria and rubrics for Lab #1 that the students must perform:

1. Was the student able to define the scope and requirements for the attack and penetration test plan? – [**20%**]
2. Was the student able to document the attack and penetration test plan scope, the major steps, the required data, and the expected data to be collected during the penetration test? – [**20%**]
3. Was the student able to analyze a targeted organization's profile and gather the preliminary reconnaissance information? – [**20%**]
4. Was the student able to design an attack and penetration test plan specific to gaining access to this organization's network? – [**20%**]
5. Was the student able to document an attack and penetration test plan on the targeted organization's network? – [**20%**]

LAB #1 – ASSESSMENT WORKSHEET

Develop an Attack and Penetration Test Plan

Course Name and Number: ___

Student Name: ___

Instructor Name: ___

Lab Due Date: ___

Overview

In this lab, you followed a scenario in which you were hired as an information systems security consultant. Your client requested a written proposal for performing a penetration test on the company's production e-commerce Web application server and the CISCO core backbone network diagramed in Figure 1.1. As part of this scenario, you researched samples of existing penetration testing methodology and then used that research to create an attack and penetration test plan with a predefined table of contents.

Lab Assessment Questions & Answers

1. Provide a brief summary of the activities in each of the hacking steps listed below.

___

2. To exploit or attack the targeted systems, what can you do as an initial first step to collect as much information as possible about the targets prior to devising an attack and penetration test plan?

___

3. What applications and tools can be used to perform this initial reconnaissance and probing step?

___

4. How can social engineering be used to gather information or data about the organization's IT infrastructure?

5. What does the enumeration step of the five-step hacking process entail and how is it vital to the hacker's objective?

6. Explain how an attacker will avoid being detected following a successful penetration attack.

7. What method does an attacker use to regain access to an already penetrated system?

8. As a security professional, you have been asked to perform an intrusive penetration test, which involves cracking into the organization's WLAN. While performing this task, you are able to retrieve the authentication key. Should you use this and continue testing, or stop here and report your findings to the client? Explain your answer.

9. Why would an organization want to conduct an internal penetration test?

10. What constitutes a situation in which a penetration tester should not compromise or access a system as part of a controlled penetration test?

11. Why would an organization hire an outside consulting firm to perform an intrusive penetration test without the IT department's knowledge?

12. How does a Web application penetration test differ from a network penetration test?

13. Explain both the information systems security practitioner and hacker perspectives for performing a penetration test.

____

____

____

____

____

Implement Hashing and Encryption for Secure Communications

LAB 2

Introduction

In this lab, you will apply common cryptographic and hashing techniques to ensure message and file transfer integrity and maximize confidentiality. You also will create an MD5sum and SHA1 hash on a sample file on the Linux virtual machine and compare the hash values of the original files with those generated after the file has been modified. Next, you will use GnuPG to generate a public key, a private key, and a secret key to encrypt and decrypt a message. You will use these keys to send secure messages between two user accounts on the virtual machine and verify the integrity of the received files. Finally, you will review the process for uploading public keys to a public PKI website.

Learning Objectives

Upon completing this lab, you will be able to:

- Apply common cryptographic and hashing techniques on a message to ensure message confidentiality and integrity
- Verify the integrity of a message or file using hashing techniques to determine if it has been manipulated or modified
- Create an MD5sum and SHA1 hash on a message or file and verify file integrity
- Relate how a change or edit to the message or file changes the hash value and why it is important to check the hash provided before executing or unzipping a binary or some other unknown file
- Encrypt and decrypt a GPG encrypted message to ensure confidentiality between two parties

TOOLS AND SOFTWARE

NAME	MORE INFORMATION
GNU Privacy Guard (GnuPG)	http://www.gnupg.org/

Deliverables

Upon completion of this lab, you are required to provide the following deliverables to your instructor:

1. A text document that includes each of the following items:
   a. MD5sum and SHA1 hash for the original example.txt file;
   b. MD5sum and SHA1 hash for the modified example.txt file;
   c. Screen capture of the encrypted file (cleartext.txt.gpg);
   d. Screen capture of the decrypted file (gpg –d cleartext.txt.gpg);
   e. Screen capture of the directory listing showing student.pub;
   f. Screen capture of the directory listing showing instructor.pub;
2. Lab Assessment Questions & Answers for Lab #2.

Hands-On Steps

1. This lab begins at the student landing vWorkstation virtual machine desktop of the VSCL, as shown here.

FIGURE 2.1

"Student Landing" VSCL workstation

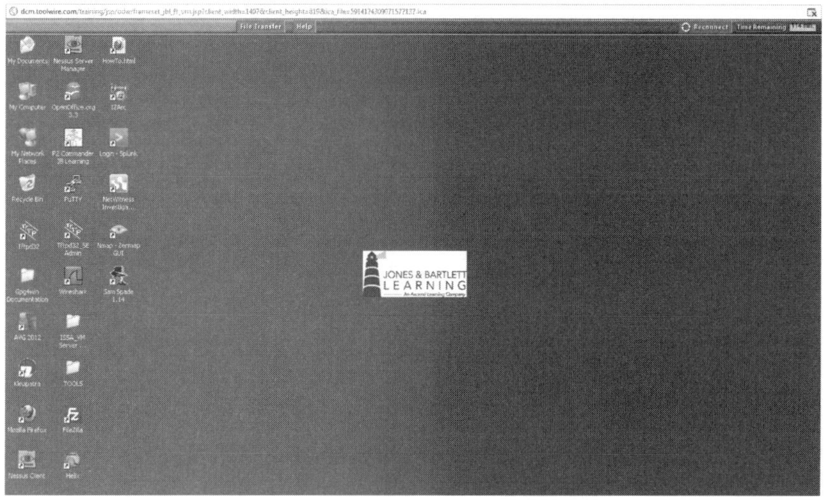

> **Note:**
>
> The next steps will create a simple text file in the student folder of the Linux virtual machine that you will use to complete the steps in this lab.

2. **Double-click** the **ISSA_VM Server Farm_RDP icon** on the desktop.
3. **Double-click** the **TargetUbuntu02 icon** to a remote desktop connection to the Linux server.

FIGURE 2.2

Open a remote desktop connection to TargetUbuntu02

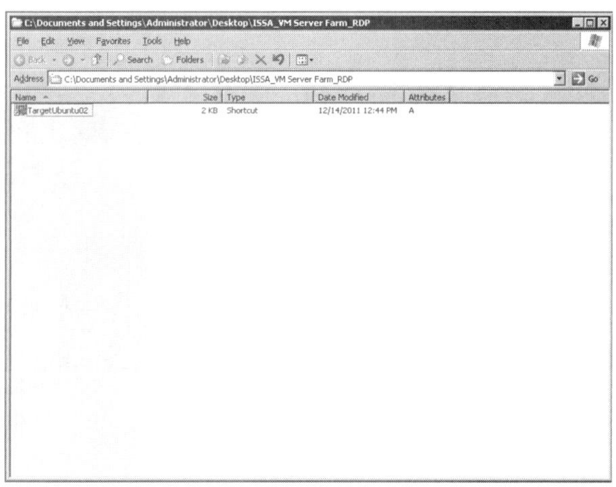

4. **Log in** to the **TargetUbuntu02 VM** server with the following credentials:
   - User name: **student**
   - Password: **ISS316Security**

FIGURE 2.3

Connecting to TargetUbuntu02 server

5. From the Linux toolbar, **click Applications** > **Accessories** > **gedit Text Editor** to open the Linux text editor.

FIGURE 2.4

Opening the gedit Text Editor

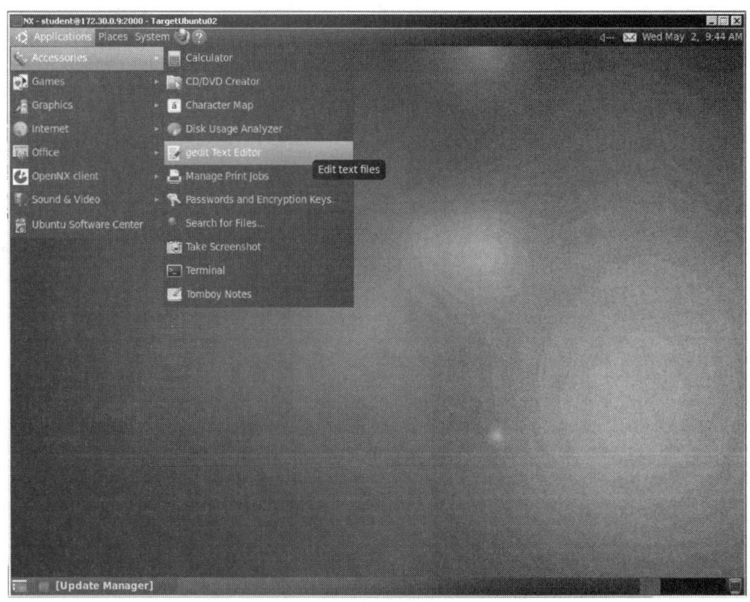

6. In the gedit window, **type This is an example.** and **click** the **Save button** on the edit toolbar.
7. In the Name box of the Save As dialog box, **type Example.txt**.
8. In the Save in folder drop-down menu, **select** the **student** folder and **press Save**.

FIGURE 2.5

Saving the Example.txt file

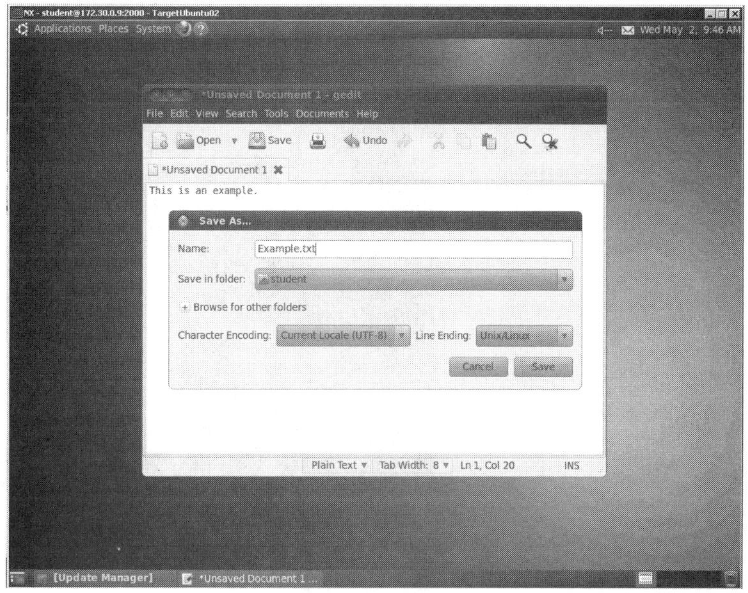

9. **Close** the **gedit window**.

Note:

The next steps will create an MD5sum hash string for a file on the Linux virtual machine. You will then verify that the addition of the MD5sum hash string did not alter the contents of the file.

10. From the Linux toolbar, **click Applications > Accessories > Terminal** to open a terminal window.
11. At the command prompt, **type man MD5sum** to open the onscreen manual for this tool.

FIGURE 2.6

Viewing the MD5sum onscreen manual

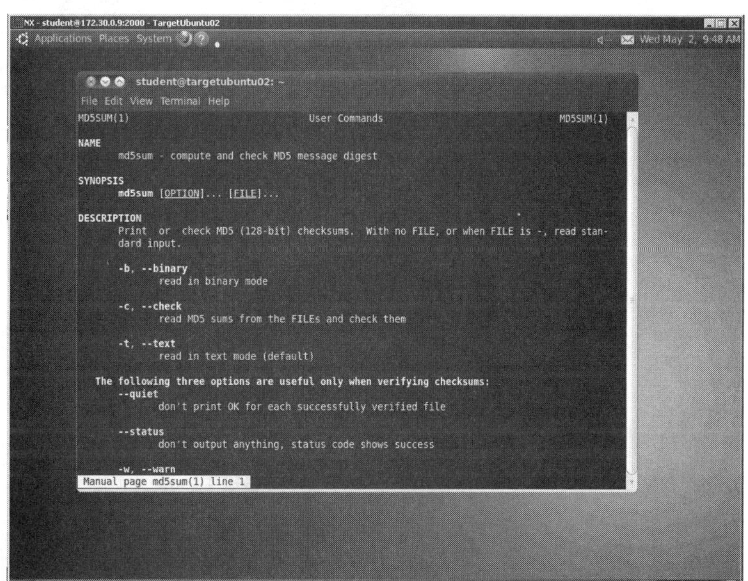

12. **Use** the **arrow keys** to explore the functions and switches for this tool.
13. At the command prompt, **type q** to exit the manual page and return to the terminal prompt.
14. At the command prompt, **type ls –l** to list the files in the student folder.

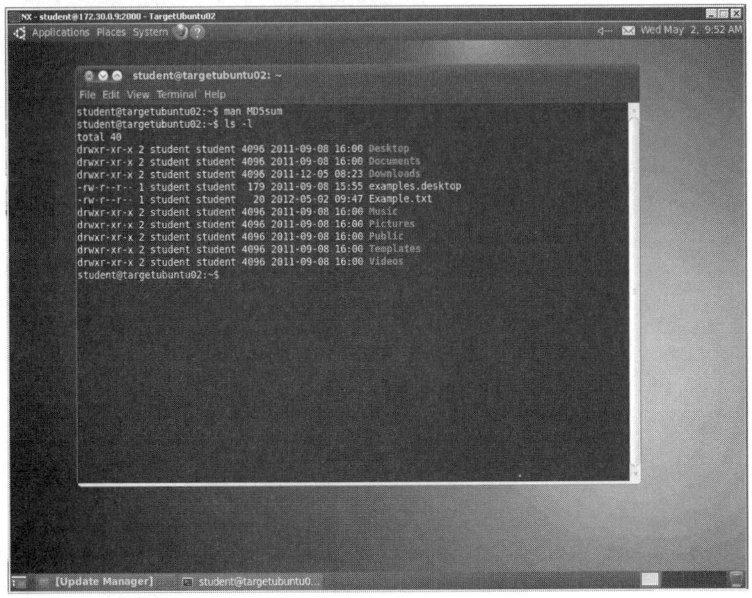

FIGURE 2.7

Listing the files in the student folder

15. At the command prompt, **type cat Example.txt** to view the contents of the Example.txt file.

    The contents of the file should be the same *This is an example.* phrase that you typed in step 6.
16. At the command prompt, **type md5sum Example.txt** to create an MD5sum hash string for the Example.txt file.

    The tool will return a string of hexadecimal numbers.

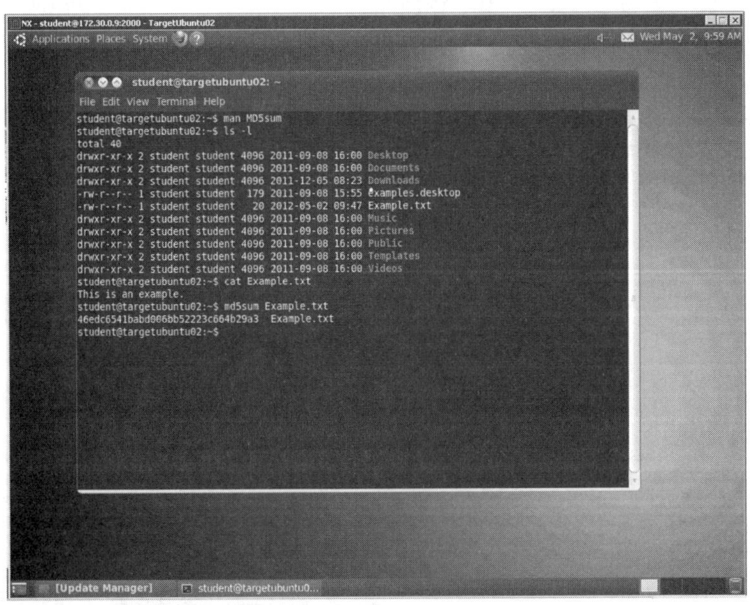

FIGURE 2.8

Generating an MD5sum hash for the Example.txt file

17. In a new text document, **record** the **MD5sum hash string**.
18. At the command prompt, **type md5sum Example.txt > Example.txt.md5** to store the MD5sum hash string with the Example.txt file.
19. At the command prompt, **type ls** to list the files in the student folder and verify that the new Example.txt.md5 file has been saved properly.

FIGURE 2.9

Verifying the contents of the student folder

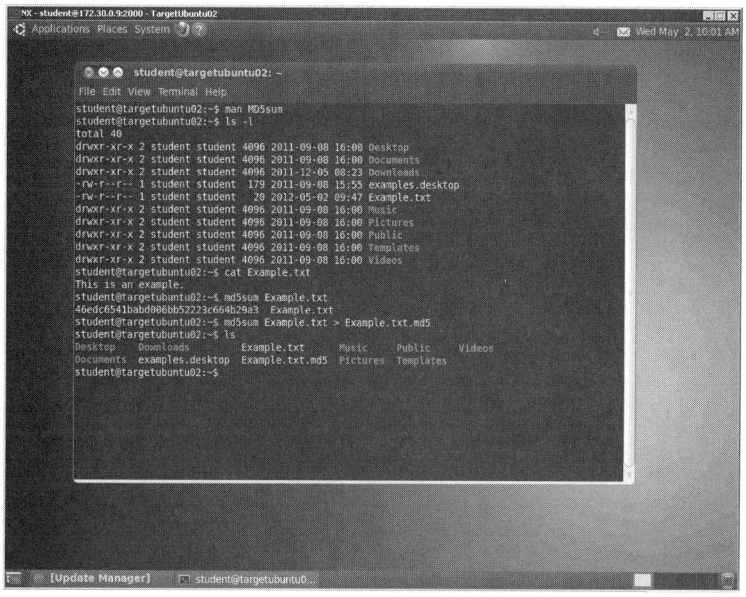

20. At the command prompt, **type cat Example.txt.md5** to view the contents of the Example.txt.md5 hashed file.

    The contents of the file should be the same MD5sum hash string that you recorded in step 17.
21. At the command prompt, **type md5sum –c Example.txt.md5** to compare the value of the hashed file with the original Example.txt file.

    If correct, the system will display the words *Example.txt: OK*, indicating that the MD5sum hash worked correctly.

FIGURE 2.10

Verifying the MD5sum hash worked correctly

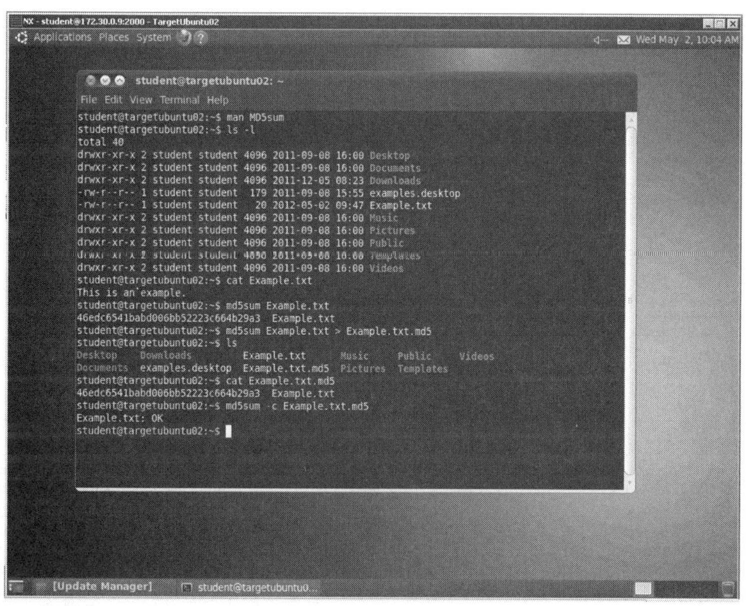

> **Note:**
> The next steps will create a SHA1sum hash string for a file on the Linux virtual machine. You will then verify that the addition of the SHA1sum hash string did not alter the file's contents.

22. At the command prompt, **type man SHA1sum** to review the onscreen manual describing the features and switches for this tool.
23. **Use** the **arrow keys** to explore the functions and switches for this tool.

FIGURE 2.11
Viewing the SHA1 onscreen manual

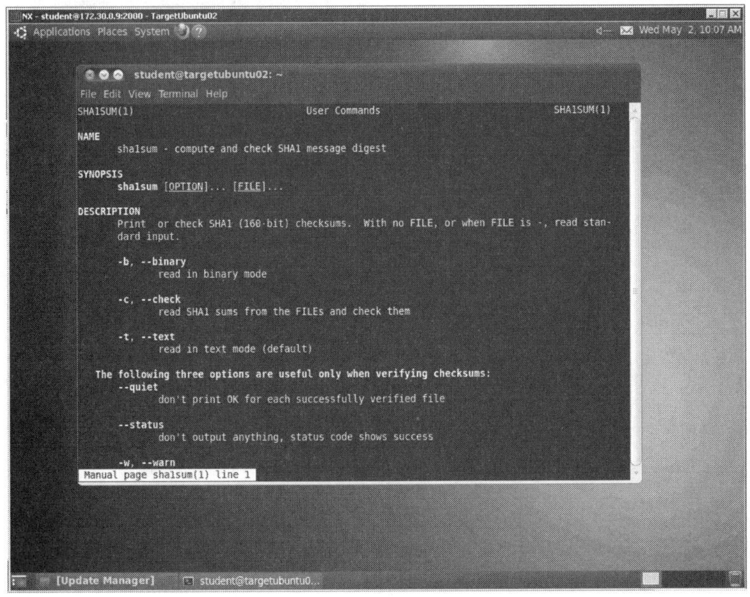

24. At the command prompt, **type q** to exit the manual page and return to the terminal prompt.
25. At the command prompt, **type sha1sum Example.txt** to create a SHA1sum hash string for the Example.txt file.

    The tool will return a string of hexadecimal numbers.

FIGURE 2.12
Generating a SHA1sum hash for the Example.txt file

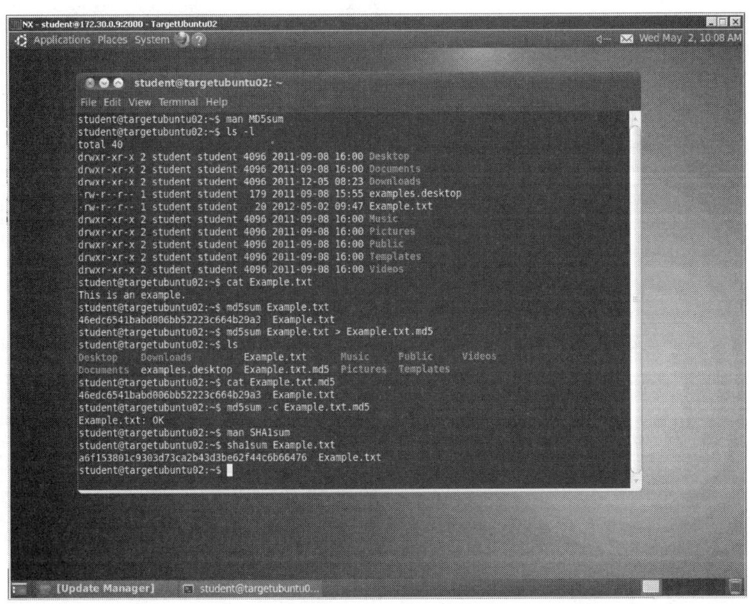

26. In your text document, **record** the **SHA1sum hash string**.
27. At the command prompt, **type sha1sum Example.txt > Example.txt.sha1** to store the SHA1sum hash string with the Example.txt file.
28. At the command prompt, **type ls** to list the files in the student folder and verify that the new Example.txt.sha1 file has been saved properly.

FIGURE 2.13

Verifying the contents of the student folder

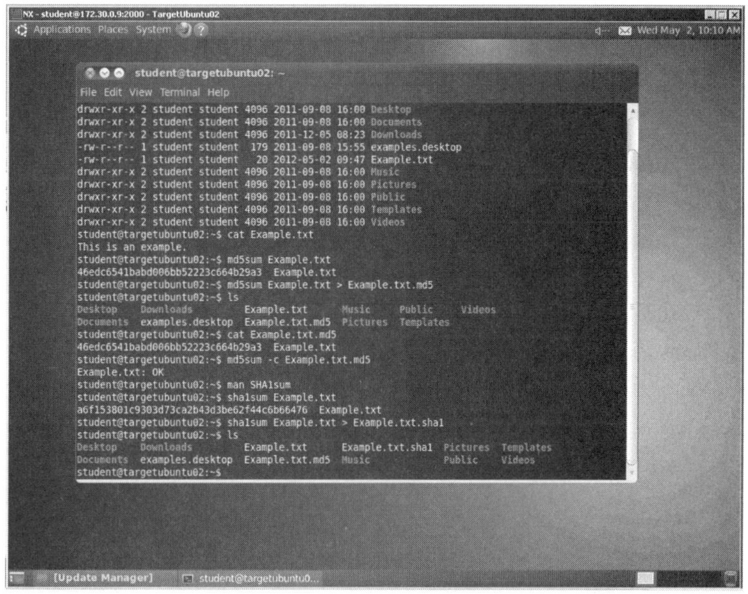

29. At the command prompt, **type cat Example.txt.sha1** to view the contents of the Example.txt.sha1 hashed file.

    The file's contents should be the same SHA1sum hash string that you recorded in step 26.
30. At the command prompt, **type sha1sum –c Example.txt.sha1** to compare the value of the hashed file with the original Example.txt file.

    If correct, the system will display the words *Example.txt: OK*, indicating that the SHA1sum hash worked correctly.

FIGURE 2.14

Verifying the SHA1sum hash worked correctly

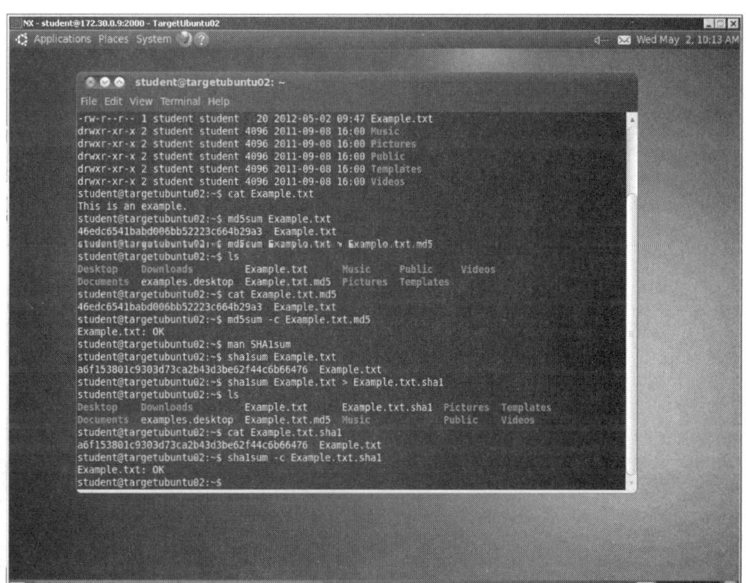

> **Note:**
> The next steps will modify the Example.txt file you created earlier in this lab. You will then repeat the steps to create an MD5sum and SHA1sum hash for the modified file and compare the hash values with those recorded for the original file.

31. At the command prompt, **type echo more text >> Example.txt** to add the words *more text* to the end of the Example.txt file modifying its contents.
32. At the command prompt, **type cat Example.txt** to view the contents of the modified file.
33. At the command prompt, **type md5sum Example.txt** to create an MD5sum hash string for the modified Example.txt file.

    The tool will return a string of hexadecimal numbers.
34. In your text document, **record** the **MD5sum hash string** for the modified Example.txt file.
35. At the command prompt, **type SHA1sum Example.txt** to create a SHA1sum hash string for the modified Example.txt file.

    The tool will return a string of hexadecimal numbers.
36. In your text document, **record** the **SHA1sum hash string** for the modified Example.txt file.
37. In your text document, **briefly explain** why this change occurred and how it could be useful to a security analyst verifying file integrity.

> **Note:**
> The next steps will use the GnuPG (Gnu Privacy Guard) to encrypt messages that you will send between two fictitious users (*Instructor* and *Student*). You will first generate a GPG key from the student account.

38. In the terminal window, **verify** that the command prompt is **student@targetubuntu02:~$**.
39. At the command prompt, **type gpg --gen-key** to generate a public encryption key.

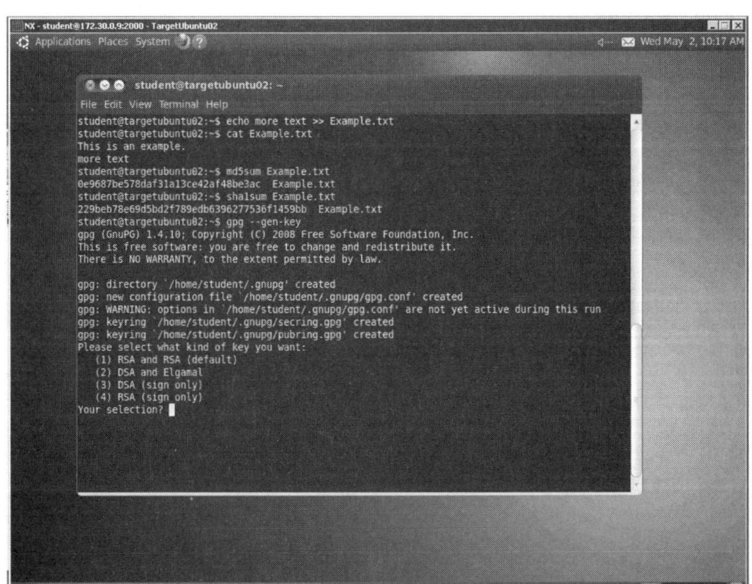

FIGURE 2.15
Generating a GPG key

40. When prompted by the key generator, **type** the following answers in response to the onscreen questions:
    - Your [key type] selection? **1** (RSA and RSA default)
    - What keysize do you want? **1024** (1024 bit length)
    - Key is valid for? **0** (Key does not expire at all)
    - Is this correct? **y** (yes)
41. When prompted by the key generator, **type** the following answers in response to the request for a user ID to identify your key:
    - Real name: **Student**
    - Email address: **student@vlabsolutions.com**
    - Comment: **press Enter**
    - Change (N)ame, (C)omment, (E)mail or (O)kay/(Q)uit?: **O**
    - Passphrase: **ISS316Security**
    - Repeat passphrase: **ISS316Security**

    The system will display an error message: *Not enough random bytes available*. You will generate more random bytes in the following steps by performing a series of actions, such as typing on the keyboard, moving the mouse, using disk space, and playing games.

FIGURE 2.16

"Not enough random bytes available" error message

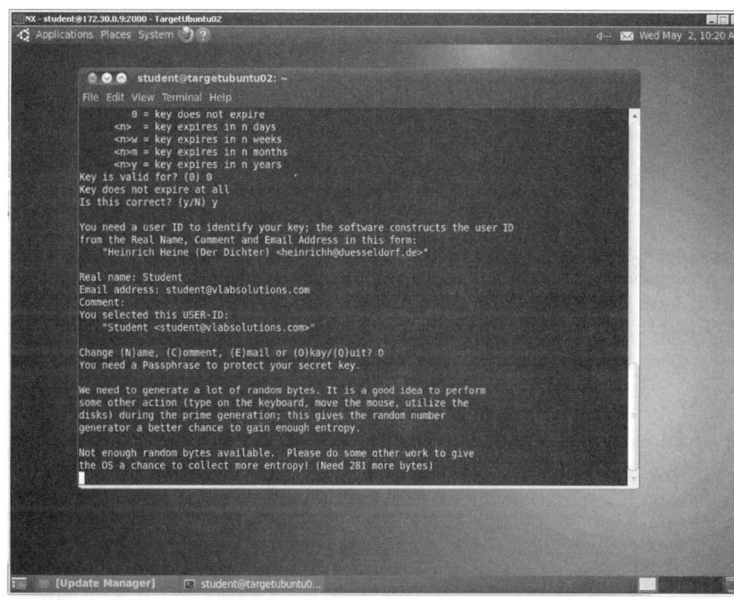

42. From the Linux toolbar, **click Applications** > **Accessories** > **Terminal** to open a second terminal window.
43. At the command prompt, **type sudo -i** to access the superuser account on **root@targetubuntu02:~$**.
44. When prompted for a password, **type ISS316Security**.
45. At the command prompt, **type dd if=/dev/zero of=5gfile bs=1G count=5** to generate some random bytes.
46. **Click** in the **first terminal window** to activate it.

47. From the Linux toolbar, **click Applications > Games > AisleRiot Solitaire** to open a session of Solitaire.

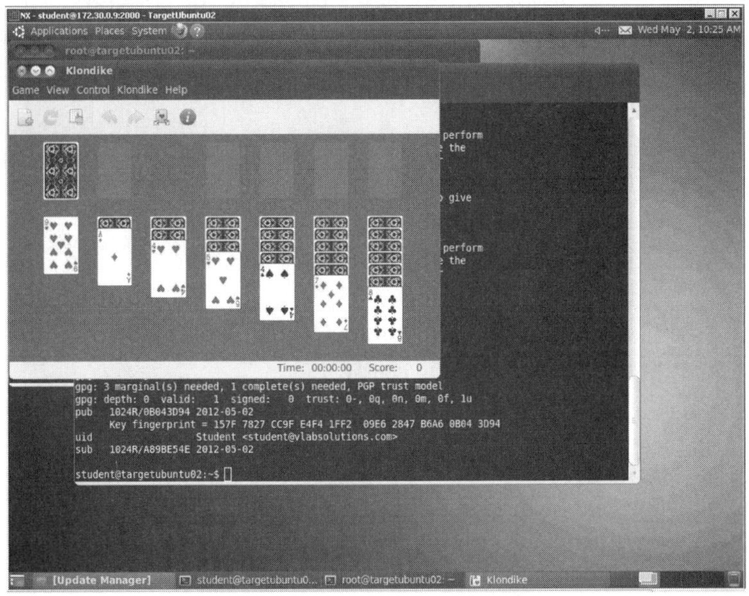

FIGURE 2.17

Generating random bytes to create the GPG key

48. **Play Solitaire** until the command prompt appears in the student@targetubuntu02:~ terminal window. The reappearance of the command prompt indicates that sufficient bytes were available to create the GPG key.
49. **Close** the **Solitaire window.**

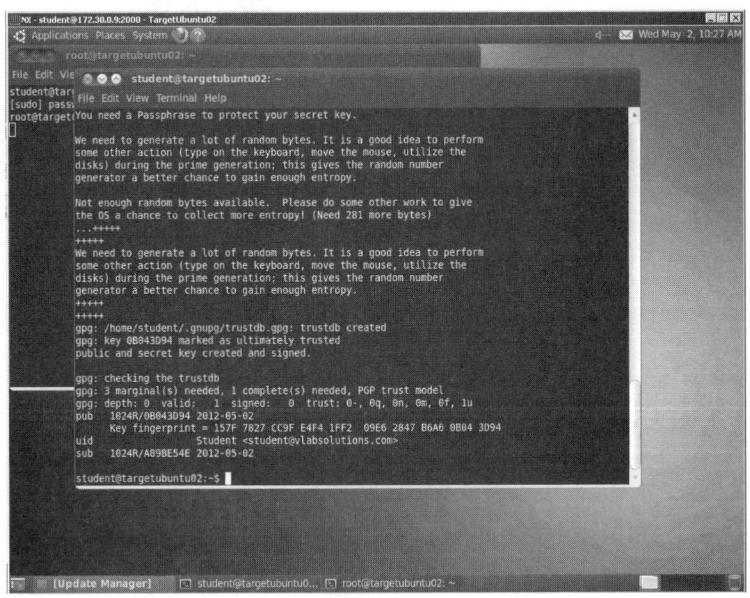

FIGURE 2.18

GPG keys for the student account

50. **Close** the **root@targetubuntu02:~ terminal window.**

51. At the command prompt in the student@targetubuntu02:~ terminal window, **type gpg --export -a > student.pub** to save the GPG key to a file called student.pub.
52. At the command prompt, **type ls** to list the files in the folder and verify that the student.pub file was saved correctly.
53. **Make a screen capture** of the displayed contents and **paste** it into your text document.

> **Note:**
> To capture the screen, **press** the **Ctrl** and **PrtSc** keys together, and then **use Ctrl + V** to paste the image into a Word or other word processor document.

> **Note:**
> The next steps will generate a GPG key from the instructor account. You will then use the GnuPG (Gnu Privacy Guard) to encrypt messages that you will send between two fictitious users (*Instructor* and *Student*).

54. To create the GPG keys for the instructor account, you must first log in to the instructor account on the Linux machine. At the command prompt, **type pwd** to determine which directory you are currently using.

    The system should display */home/student* indicating that you are in the student folder. If you see something else on your display, change to that directory before continuing.
55. At the command prompt, **type whoami** to verify that you are still logged in to the student account.

    The system should display *student* indicating that you are logged in to the student account. If you see something else on your display, contact your instructor.
56. At the command prompt, **type su instructor** to switch to the instructor account.
57. When prompted for a password, **type ISS316Security**.
58. At the command prompt, **type cd /home/instructor** to change directories to the instructor folder.
59. At the command prompt, **type ls** to list the contents of the instructor folder.

Implement Hashing and Encryption for Secure Communications 2

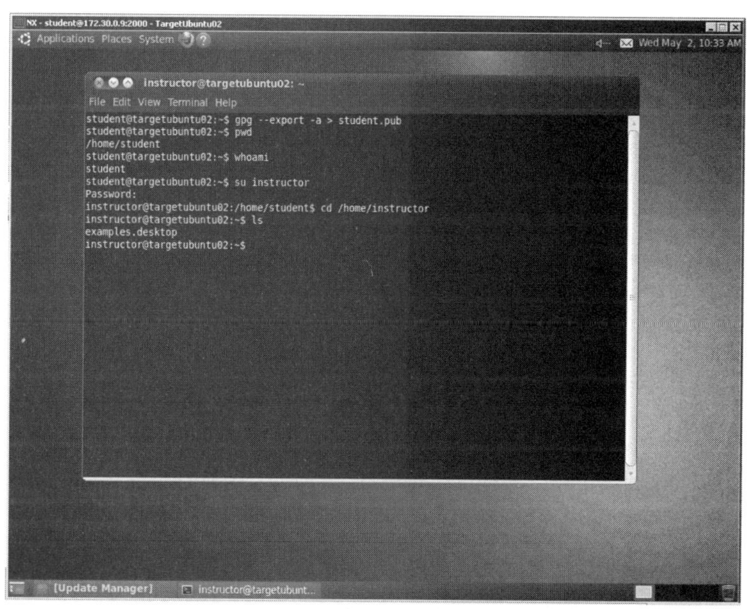

FIGURE 2.19
The contents of the instructor folder

60. **Repeat steps 39-50** to create the GPG keys for the instructor account. Note the following change to step 41:
    - Real name: **Instructor**
    - Email address: **instructor@vlabsolutions.com**

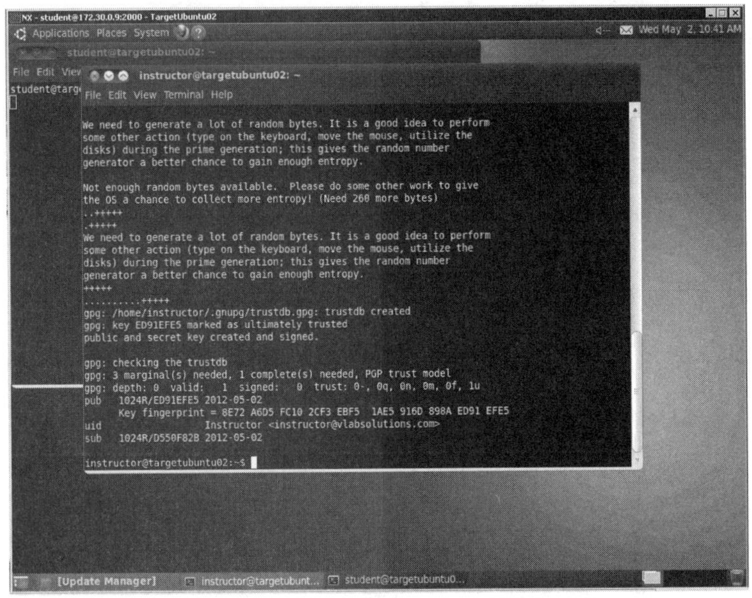

FIGURE 2.20

GPG keys for the instructor account

61. At the command prompt in the instructor@targetubuntu02:~ terminal window, **type gpg ––export –a > instructor.pub** to save the GPG key to a file called instructor.pub.
62. At the command prompt, **type ls** to list the files in the folder and verify that the instructor.pub file was saved correctly.
63. **Make a screen capture** of the displayed contents and **paste** it into your text document.
64. At the command prompt, **type exit** to return to using the student account.

    The command prompt should change to *student@targetubuntu02:~$*.
65. At the command prompt, **type whoami** to verify that you are using the student account.

    The system should display *student*, indicating that you are logged in to the student account.

> **Note:**
> The next steps will share the GPG keys you just created between the *Instructor* and *Student* accounts. This step ensures that a file or message encrypted by a sender (*Student*) can be decrypted by the recipient (*Instructor*).

66. At the command prompt, **type sudo cp /home/instructor/instructor.pub instructor.pub** to copy the instructor GPG keys (instructor.pub) to the student folder.
67. When prompted for a password, **type ISS316Security**.

68. At the command prompt, **type ls** to list the contents of the student folder and verify that the instructor.pub file is now included.

FIGURE 2.21

Viewing the contents of the student folder

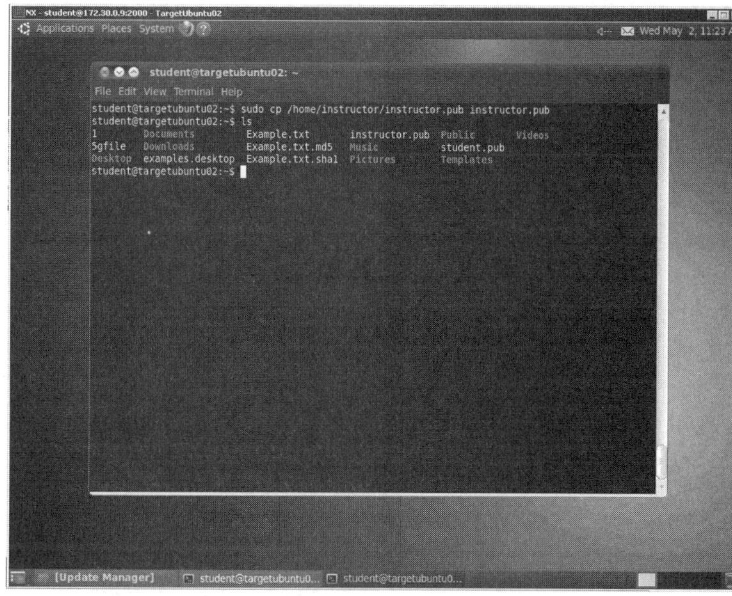

69. At the command prompt, **type gpg --list-keys** to list the current public key ring for the student account.
70. At the command prompt, **type gpg --import instructor.pub** to import the instructor's GPG keys to the student public key ring.
71. At the command prompt, **type gpg --list-keys** to list the current public key ring for the student account.

FIGURE 2.22

Exchanging public GPG keys

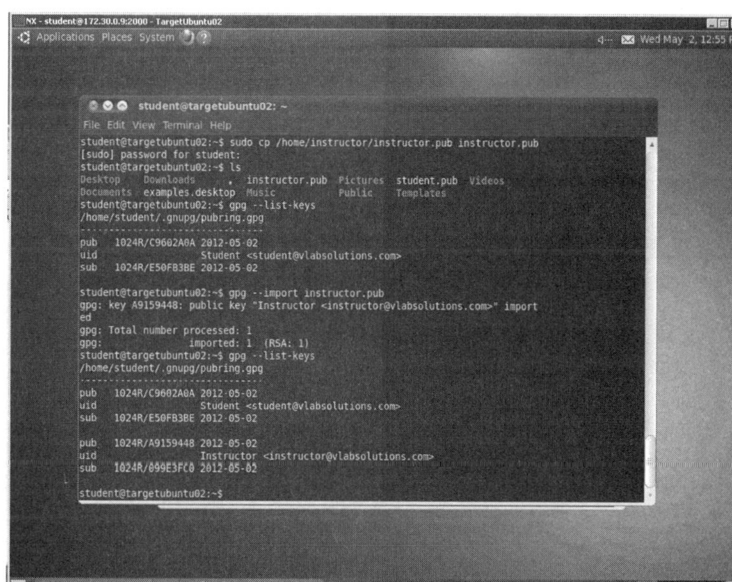

Note:
The next steps will use the GPG keys you've already exchanged to encrypt and decrypt a cleartext message that you will send between the two users (*Instructor* and *Student*). You will first need to create the message, and then apply encryption.

72. At the command prompt, **type echo "this is a clear-text message" > cleartext.txt** to create a new message.
73. At the command prompt, **type cat cleartext.txt** to view the contents of the message.

FIGURE 2.23

Viewing the contents of the message

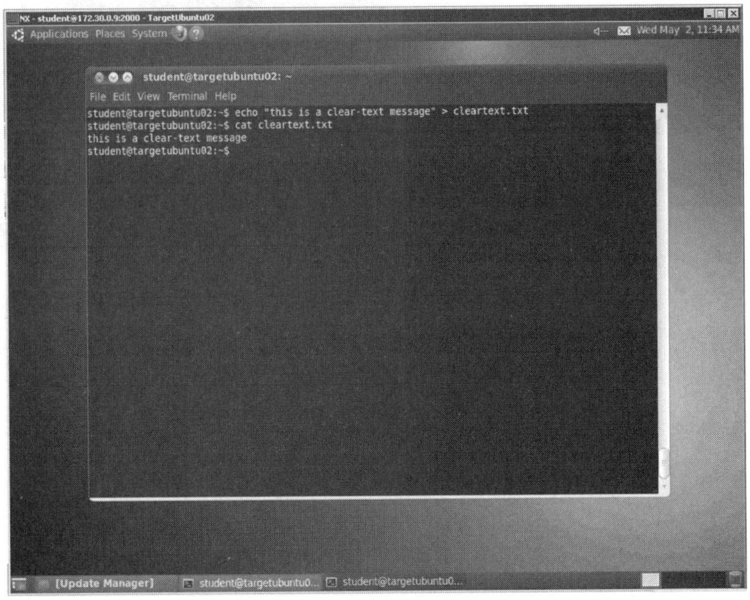

74. At the command prompt **type gpg –e cleartext.txt > cleartext.txt** to encrypt the message.
75. When prompted by the encryption process, **type** the following responses:
    - Enter the [recipient] user ID: **instructor**
    - Use this key anyway?: **y**
    - End with an empty line: press **Enter**
76. At the command prompt **type ls** to list the contents of the folder and verify that the encrypted file (cleartext.txt.gpg) has been created.
77. At the command prompt **type cat cleartext.txt.gpg** to view the contents of the file and verify that it is encrypted.

FIGURE 2.24

Viewing an encrypted file

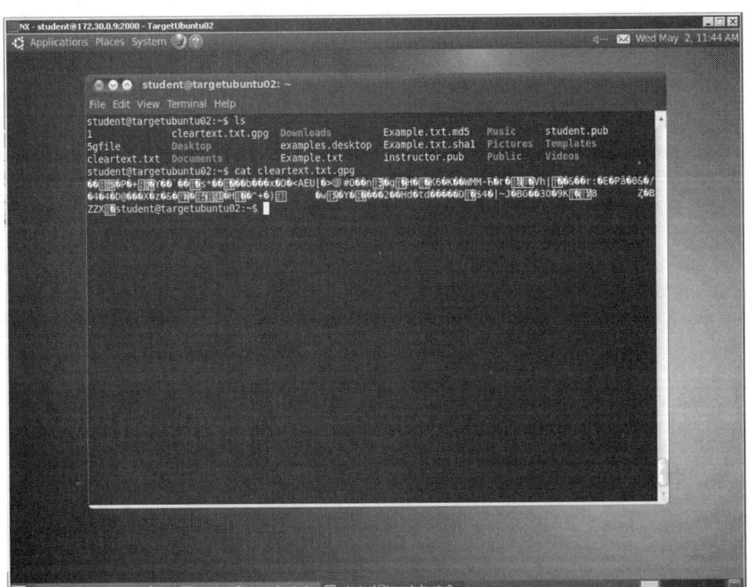

78. **Make a screen capture** of the displayed contents and **paste** it into your text document.
79. To decrypt the message, begin by switching to the instructor account. **Type su instructor** at the command prompt.
80. When prompted for a password, **type ISS316Security**.
    The command prompt should change to *instructor@targetubuntu02:~/home/student$*.
81. At the command prompt, **type whoami** to verify that you are now using the instructor account.
    The system should display *instructor* indicating that you are logged in to the instructor account.
82. At the command prompt, **type gpg –d cleartext.txt.gpg** to decrypt the message.
83. When prompted for the GPG passphrase, **type ISS316Security**.
    The system will display the contents of the decrypted message.

FIGURE 2.25
Viewing the decrypted file

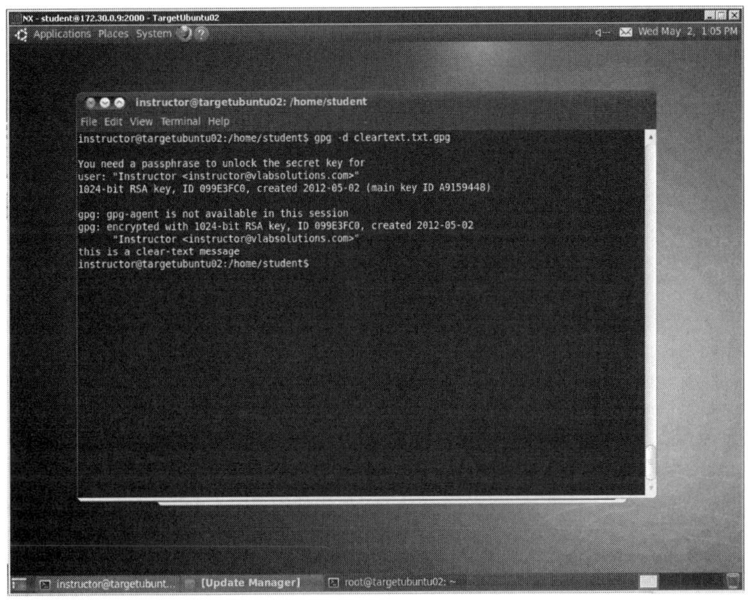

84. **Make a screen capture** of the displayed contents and **paste** it into your text document.
85. At the command prompt, **type exit** to return to the student account.
86. Use the **File Transfer button** to download the **text file** to your local computer and submit it as part of your deliverables.

> **Note:**
> The next steps will explore how to sign a public key and then upload that key to an online site (http://pgp.mit.edu). You will not actually upload these keys.

87. At the command prompt, **type man gpg** to view the onscreen manual for the GPG tool and review the information about signing a key.
88. **Use** the **arrow keys** to explore the functions and switches for this tool.
89. At the command prompt, **type q** to exit the manual page and return to the terminal prompt.
90. From a machine with an Internet connection, open an Internet browser application and **type http://pgp.mit.edu** in the browser's address box.
91. **Review** the links in the Help section of the page to see the requirements for uploading a key to the MIT PGP Public Key Server. You will use this information in a deliverable for this lab.

Evaluation Criteria and Rubrics

The following are the evaluation criteria and rubrics for Lab #2 that students must perform:

1. Was the student able to apply common cryptographic and hashing techniques on a message to ensure message confidentiality and integrity? – [20%]
2. Was the student able to verify the integrity of a message or file using hashing tools to determine if it has been manipulated or modified? – [20%]
3. Was the student able to create an MD5sum and SHA1 hash on a message or file and verify file integrity? – [20%]
4. Was the student able to relate how a change or edit to the message or file changes the hash value and why it is important to check the hash provided before executing or unzipping a binary or some other unknown file? – [20%]
5. Was the student able to encrypt and decrypt a GPG encrypted message to ensure confidentiality between two parties? – [20%]

LAB #2 – ASSESSMENT WORKSHEET

Implement Hashing and Encryption for Secure Communications

Course Name and Number: ______________________________

Student Name: ______________________________

Instructor Name: ______________________________

Lab Due Date: ______________________________

Overview

In this lab, you applied common cryptographic and hashing techniques to ensure message and file transfer integrity and maximize confidentiality. You also created an MD5sum and SHA1 hash on a sample file on the Linux virtual machine and compared the hash values of the original files with those generated after the file had been modified. Next, you used GnuPG to generate a public key, a private key, and a secret key to encrypt and decrypt a message. You then used these keys to send secure messages between two user accounts on the virtual machine and verify the integrity of the received files. Finally, you reviewed the process for uploading public keys to a public PKI website.

Lab Assessment Questions & Answers

1. Compare the hash values calculated for *example.txt* that you documented during this lab. Explain in your own words why the hash values will change when the data is modified.

____
____
____
____
____
____

2. Why are the MD5sum and SHA1sum hash values the same every time you calculate for the "example.txt" sample file? What if they were different when you re-calculated the hash value at the other end?

____
____
____

3. If you were using corporate e-mail for internal and external communications but did not want to encrypt an e-mail message, what other security countermeasure can you deploy to ensure message integrity?

4. If you are using corporate e-mail for external communications that contain confidential information, what other security countermeasure can you deploy to maximize confidentiality of e-mail transmissions through the Internet?

5. What is the difference between MD5sum and SHA1sum hashing calculations? Which is better and why?

6. Where can you store your public keys or public certificate files in the public domain? Is this the same thing as a public key infrastructure (PKI) server?

7. What do you need if you want to decrypt encrypted messages and files from a trusted sender?

8. Do you recommend that end-users encrypt their personal hard drives?

9. What happens if you have a forensic copy of a hard drive that happens to have the entire disk encrypted that you try to view with standard forensic tools?

Perform Data Gathering and Footprinting on a Targeted Website

LAB 3

Introduction

The first phase of hacking is the footprinting phase, which is designed to passively gain information about a target. In this lab, you will identify a target organization with an Internet website and perform data gathering and footprinting for the site using Internet search tools. You will collect public domain information about the organization's website by making use of Google hacking techniques, downloading the Sam Spade reconnaissance-gathering tool, and using *nslookup* and *tracert*, similar DOS command tools packages with Microsoft® Windows. You also will research public domain sites such as IANA's WHOIS tool to obtain public domain information about the targeted website. Finally, you will record the information you uncover in a research paper, describing how this information can make an organization vulnerable to hackers.

The purpose of this lab is to share common techniques used by both black- and white-hat hackers to expose vulnerabilities. As such, you should recognize that as with any hacking activity, it may take several tries to uncover a truly vulnerable organization. Many organizations closely monitor their websites for any activity that might indicate hacking. Know too, that Google hacking does not work on every site on the Internet and that sometimes the best results come from smaller, local companies that are less likely to employ effective monitoring.

This lab is a paper-based design lab and does not require use of the Virtual Security Cloud Lab (VSCL). To successfully complete the deliverables for this lab, you will need access to a text editor or word processor, such as Microsoft® Word. For some labs, you may also need access to a graphics line drawing application, such as Visio or PowerPoint.

> **Note:**
> If you don't have a word processor or graphics package, use OpenOffice on the student landing vWorkstation for your lab deliverables and to answer the lab assessment questions. To capture screenshots, **press Prt Sc > MSPAINT, paste** into a text document, and **save** the document in the Security_Strategies folder (**C:\Security_Strategies**) using the File Transfer function.

Learning Objectives and Outcomes

Upon completing this lab, you will be able to:

- Perform live data gathering and footprinting of a targeted organization and its website
- Gather valuable public domain information about the targeted organization and its website
- Assess what information is available publicly and what information should not be in the public domain for that organization
- Perform Google hacking research to identify known user logons and passwords and other website vulnerabilities
- Write a summary of findings reconnaissance report describing the data gathered and footprint information collected in the public domain for a targeted organization

Deliverables

Upon completion of this lab, you are required to provide the following deliverables to your instructor:

1. Hacking Lab #3 Data Gathering and Footprinting Research Report;
2. Lab Assessment Questions & Answers for Lab #3.

Hands-On Steps

1. This lab begins at a workstation with Internet access. **Double-click** any **Internet browser icon** on your desktop to open the application.
2. **Select** a **target organization** with an e-commerce website. You can target an organization with which you are already familiar, or use the browser's search tool to identify a potential target organization.
3. In a new text document, **create** a **Hacking Lab #3 Data Gathering and Footprinting Research Report.**

   You will follow the steps in this lab to complete the research report as if you were gathering information for a potential attack. You will be responsible for determining what to document in this report.

> **Note:**
> The next steps will guide you through the steps you will take to capture data that might be useful in performing a potential attack on a corporate website. You will be directed to select a company to investigate via Google, including attempting to browse password or admin directories on their web server.

4. In your browser's address box, **type google.com** to open the Google search tool.
5. Using Google as your search engine, **locate** the following information and **record** it in your text document:
   - Name of the target organization
   - Domain name and extension (*domain.ext)* for the target organization (for example, target.com)
   - URLs for the e-commerce website and any social networking sites
   - Physical address of each location used by the target company; use Google map to locate those buildings
   - Names of officers (for example, CEO, president, and CIO) at the organization
   - Number of employees at each physical location
   - Business partners or clients of the organization

   Select a company that has a simple enough organizational structure that you can attempt to document all of the information requested in that step. If you were to choose a large company, like Cisco for example, it would be very difficult to find all of their physical office locations or even estimate how many employees they have. Selecting a smaller company will make this more feasible. Remember that the objective of this step is to see how much you can learn about an organization simply by Googling it—you might be surprised at how much you can find, but do not be overwhelmed if there are some components of that lab step that you can't find responses for.

> **Note:**
> The next steps will attempt Google hacking commands on your chosen organization's website. Recognize that some organizations block directory browsing on their web server, in which case, you'll be redirected to basic Google search results about your chosen organization.

6. In the Google search box, **type site: *domain.ext* index of /password** and **press Search**, using the domain name and extension you recorded in step 5.

   This type of query in Google will return information about the target organization's Web server or applications, including any of the following:
   - A traversable directory structure that allows you to see sensitive files or configuration information by browsing the directory structure
   - A vulnerable Web-based application or applications that allow cross-site scripting
   - A vulnerable Web-based application that allows SQL injection using a UNION statement or similar exploit

7. In your text document, **record** any useful information you find using this Google hacking query. You may choose to **make** a **screen capture** of the data and **paste** it into your text document.

> **Note:**
> To capture the screen, **press** the **Ctrl** and **PrtSc** keys together, and then **use Ctrl + V** to paste the image into a Word or other word processor document.

8. In the Google search box, **type site: *domain.ext* index of +passwd** and **press Search**.
9. In your text document, **record** any useful information you find using this Google hacking query. You may choose to **make** a **screen capture** of the data and **paste** it into your text document.
10. In the Google search box, **type site: *domain.ext* index of /admin** and **press Search**.
11. In your text document, **record** any useful information you find using this Google hacking query. You may choose to **make** a **screen capture** of the data and **paste** it into your text document.
12. In the Google search box, **type inurl: *domain.ext* /admin** and **press Search**.
13. In your text document, **record** any useful information you find using this Google hacking query. You may choose to **make** a **screen capture** of the data and **paste** it into your text document.

> **Note:**
> If you were unable to find a vulnerable website with the Google hacking searches in the previous set of steps, the next steps see how Google hacking could work in a general sense. You can do this by simply repeating steps 6-13 without the **"site: *domain.ext*"** portion of the search query. For example, repeat step 6 as: In the Google search box, **type index of /password** and **press Search**.
>
> In addition, two new steps follow that search a company's URL for administrative folders or intranet content. You will still need to sift through the Google search results to find a website that has directory browsing open, but you should be able to find a few that will let you access and click through their web server's directory structure. Remember to record your findings with a screen capture and a description of the importance of that finding.

14. In the Google search box, **type intitle:intranet inurl:intranet+intext:"human resources"** and **press Search**.

    This query searches for human resources pages with an intranet site, which might reveal information intended only for a company's employees.
15. In your text document, **record** any useful information you find using this Google hacking query. You may choose to **make a screen capture** of the data and **paste** it into your text document.
16. In the Google search box, **type intitle:index of inurl:"/admin/*"** and **press Search**.

    This query searches for any website that has an index page and then looks for a folder called admin.
17. In your text document, **record** any useful information you find using this Google hacking query. You may choose to **make a screen capture** of the data and **paste** it into your text document.

> **Note:**
> The next steps will use the WHOIS Service will return information about the registered owner of the website, usually a registry service, such as Verisign or Public Interest Registry, and even IP addresses.

18. In your browser's address box, **type http://www.iana.org/cgi-bin/whois** to open the Internet Assigned Numbers Authority Website.
19. On the IANA WHOIS Service homepage, **type *domain.ext*** and **press Submit**.

    The WHOIS Service will return information about the registered owner of the website, usually a registry service, such as Verisign or Public Interest Registry.

20. In your text document, **record** the URL found in the **refer section** of the results of your WHOIS search.

    If your search results include information about the target company, instead of the registry service, skip to step 23.

21. In your browser's address box, **type *the URL found in the refer section*** to open the registry service's website and follow the onscreen instructions to open the registry service's WHOIS page.
22. On the registry service's WHOIS page, **type *domain.ext*** and **press Submit**.

    The registry service will return information about the domain's owner, including contact names, numbers, and addresses, and the names of associated servers.

23. In your text document, **record** any useful information you find using this query. You may choose to **make a screen capture** of the data and **paste** it into your text document.

> **Note:**
> The next steps will use the Sam Spade utility to gather DNS server information by crawling vulnerable websites to get email addresses and links to other web servers. If you do not have a Windows workstation, or cannot install the Sam Spade utility, skip to step 30.

24. In your browser's address box, **type http://www.pcworld.com/product/947049/sam-spade.html** to find the download page for the Sam Spade utility.
25. **Click** the **Sam Spade link** in the search results area of the Web page.
26. **Click** the **Download Now button**.
27. Follow the onscreen instructions to **install Sam Spade** on your Windows workstation.

    If you do not have a Windows workstation or cannot install the Sam Spade utility, skip to step 25.

28. Once installed, **click Tools** from the Sam Spade menu and test each of the tools that come with this tool on the target organization.
29. In your text document, **record** all of the **data** uncovered by the Sam Spade tools.

> **Note:**
> If you were unable to install the Sam Spade utility, the next steps will use two tools native to Microsoft Windows to uncover similar information.

30. **Click** the **Windows Start button**.
31. **Select Run** from the menu.

    If you do not have Run on the menu, **type cmd** in the Search programs and files box on the menu and **press Enter**. **Click cmd.exe** in the resulting programs list and skip to step 33.

32. **Type cmd** in the dialog box and **click OK**.
33. In the Windows Command Prompt window, **type nslookup** and **press Enter** to open the tool.
34. At the command prompt, **type set type=any** and **press Enter** to instruct the tool to return any information it uncovers.
35. At the command prompt, **type *domain.ext*** and **press Enter** to perform the nslookup search on your target organization.

36. In your text document, **record** all of the **data** uncovered by the nslookup tool. You may choose to **make** a **screen capture** of the data and **paste** it into your text document.
37. At the command prompt, **type tracert *domain.ext*** and **press Enter** to perform a trace route search on your target organization.
38. In your text document, **record** all of the **data** uncovered by the tracert tool. You may choose to **make** a **screen capture** of the data and **paste** it into your text document.
39. In your text document, **draft** a **Social Networking section** that will describe how you will use the information you gathered during this lab, and the information you would still need to obtain to plan an attack using social engineering tactics.
40. **Submit** the **text document** to your instructor as a deliverable for this lab.

Evaluation Criteria and Rubrics

The following are the evaluation criteria and rubrics for Lab #3 that the students must perform:

1. Was the student able to perform live data gathering and footprinting of a targeted organization and its website? – [**20%**]
2. Was the student able to gather valuable public domain information about the targeted organization and its website? – [**20%**]
3. Was the student able to assess what information is available publicly and what information should not be in the public domain for that organization? – [**20%**]
4. Was the student able to perform Google hacking research to identify useful known user logons and passwords and other website vulnerabilities? – [**20%**]
5. Was the student able to write a summary of findings reconnaissance report describing the data gathered and footprint information collected in the public domain for a targeted organization? – [**20%**]

LAB #3 – ASSESSMENT WORKSHEET

Perform Data Gathering and Footprinting on a Targeted Website

Course Name and Number: ______________________________

Student Name: ______________________________

Instructor Name: ______________________________

Lab Due Date: ______________________________

Overview

The first phase of hacking is the footprinting phase, which is designed to passively gain information about a target. In this lab, you identified a target organization with an Internet website and performed data gathering and footprinting for the site using Internet search tools. You collected public domain information about the organization's website by making use of Google hacking techniques, downloading the Sam Spade reconnaissance-gathering tool, and using *nslookup* and *tracert*, similar DOS command tools packages with Microsoft® Windows. You also researched public domain sites such as IANA's WHOIS tool to obtain public domain information about the targeted website. Finally, you recorded the information you uncovered in a research paper, describing how this information can make an organization vulnerable to hackers.

Lab Assessment Questions & Answers

1. Which reconnaissance tool comes with Microsoft® Windows that can provide reconnaissance-gathering data and can be initiated from the DOS command prompt? What useful information does this query provide?

____

____

____

____

____

2. What information can you obtain by using the WHOIS tool? Is the IANA tool the only one you encountered during your research?

____

____

____

____

3. Besides those covered in this lab, what other functions did you discover are possible with the Sam Spade utility?

4. What is the purpose of the *tracert* command? What useful information does the trace route tool provide? How can this information be used to attack the targeted website?

5. How many different WHOIS profiles are pre-loaded in the Sam Spade utility?

6. Is Sam Spade an intrusive tool? What is your perspective on the use of a freeware utility such as Sam Spade?

7. What do you think companies and organizations should do with regard to access to WHOIS information in the public domain?

8. What icon or function in Sam Spade downloads the entire HTML code of the targeted website?

9. How can you estimate the number of employees who work in an organization's remote office or facility?

10. What is the goal when trying to use a search engine for data gathering or footprinting?

11. What is Google hacking?

Compromise and Exploit a Vulnerable Microsoft® Workstation

LAB 4

Introduction

In this lab, you will explore all five phases of hacking: reconnaissance (using Zenmap GUI for Nmap), scanning (using Nessus®), enumeration (identifying vulnerabilities), compromise (attack and exploit the known vulnerabilities using BackTrack4 Live CD and the Metasploit Framework application), and post-attack and fallback activities (recommend specific countermeasures for remediating the vulnerabilities and eliminating the exploits).

Learning Objectives

Upon completing this lab, you will be able to:

- Perform reconnaissance and probing using Zenmap GUI to identify live hosts and their common ports, services, and applications running in production
- Perform a vulnerability scan on the identified IP hosts and Microsoft® workstations using Nessus®
- Identify software vulnerabilities from the vulnerability assessment scan report and the CVE listing for this vulnerability
- Exploit the known software vulnerability using the BackTrack4 Live CD tool and Metasploit Framework to attack a known Microsoft® vulnerable workstation
- Recommend specific security countermeasures for the vulnerable Microsoft® workstation based on the results of the vulnerability assessment findings and system compromise

TOOLS AND SOFTWARE	
NAME	**MORE INFORMATION**
BackTrack	http://www.backtrack-linux.org/
Metasploit	http://www.metasploit.com
Nessus®	http://www.Nessus.org/products/Nessus
Zenmap GUI	http://nmap.org/zenmap/

Deliverables

Upon completion of this lab, you are required to provide the following deliverables to your instructor:

1. A text document containing the following items:
   a. A list of all open ports discovered by the Zenmap scan;
   b. A screen capture of the MS08-067 vulnerability described by Nessus®;
   c. A screen capture of the successful exploit on WindowsVulnerable01;
   d. A screen capture of the MS Bulletin for remediating MS08-067;
2. The HTML version of the Nessus® Lab #4 Vulnerability Scan report of WindowsVulnerable01;
3. The Microsoft® software security patch for MS08-067;
4. Lab Assessment Questions & Answers for Lab #4.

Hands-On Steps

1. This lab begins at the student landing vWorkstation virtual machine desktop of the VSCL, as shown here.

FIGURE 4.1

"Student Landing" VSCL workstation

> **Note:**
> The next steps will use the Zenmap GUI to perform reconnaissance probing on an IP address range, performing an IP discovery on the targeted IP range.

2. **Double-click** the **ISSA_VM Server Farm_RDP icon** on the desktop. This folder contains links to the virtual servers in this lab environment.
3. **Double-click** the **WindowsVulnerable01.rdp file** to open the vulnerable workstation.

   If the system displays a Remote Desktop Connection Security Warning dialog box, **click** the **OK button** to continue.

FIGURE 4.2

Open a remote connection to the WindowsVulnerable01 workstation

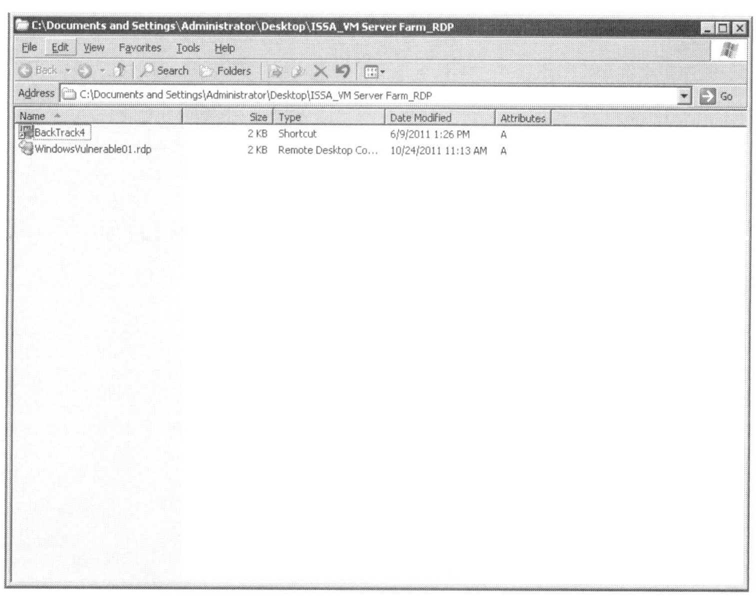

4. **Log on** to the **WindowsVulnerable01** workstation with the following credentials:
   - User name: **administrator**
   - Password: **ISS316Security**
5. From the vWorkstation desktop, click the **Windows Start button**, if necessary.
6. **Select Run** from the menu.
7. **Type cmd** in the dialog box and **click OK** to open the Windows command prompt.
8. In the Windows command prompt window, **type ipconfig** and **press Enter** to identify the IP address for this workstation.

FIGURE 4.3

Identifying the IP address

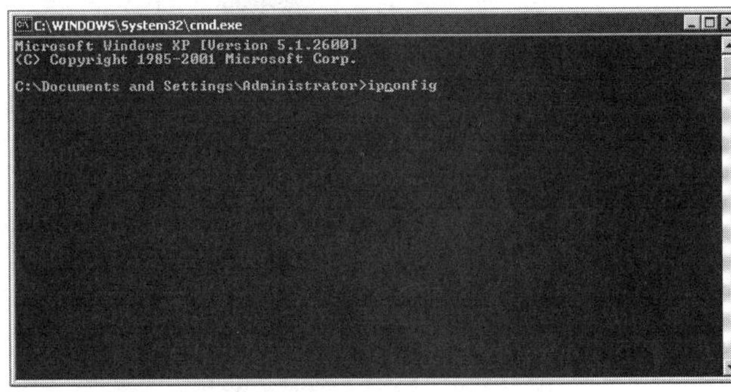

9. **Record** the **IP address** (*IP address=*________________________). You will need this information in a later step.
10. **Minimize** the **WindowsVulnerable01 window** to return to the vWorkstation desktop.
11. **Double-click** the **Nmap-Zenmap GUI icon** on the desktop.
12. From the **Target drop-down menu**, **type IP address**, using the IP address you recorded in step 9.
13. **Select Intense Scan, all TCP ports** from the **Profile drop-down menu** and **click** the **Scan button.**

    This scan can take several minutes to complete all of the test scripts. When the scan has finished, Zenmap will display the **Nmap done** command.

FIGURE 4.4

Intense Scan, all TCP ports for WindowsVulnerable01

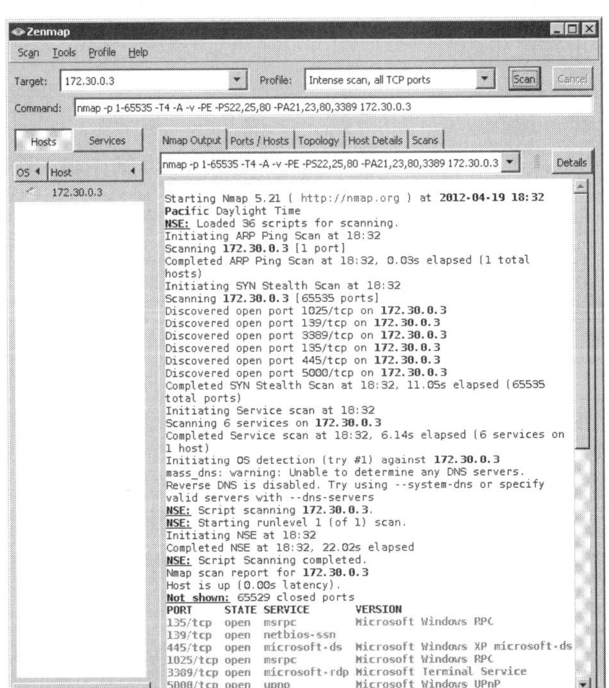

14. **Review** the **results** of the Intense scan to identify any open ports.
15. In a new text document, **record** the **list of open ports** discovered during the scan.
16. **Close** the **application window**.

> **Note:**
> The next steps will use the data collected from Zenmap GUI to perform a Nessus® vulnerability scan on the targeted WindowsVulnerable01 vWorkstation that was discovered during the port scan in the previous section. First, you will create a new user account with administrative privileges and then create a new policy definition.

17. **Double-click** the **Nessus Server Manager icon** to launch the application.

    The Nessus Server Manager will indicate that the service is running. If the service is stopped, **click** the **Start Nessus Server button** to restart the service.
18. **Click** the **Manage Users button** on the Nessus Server Manager window to add a new user account.

FIGURE 4.5

Connecting to Nessus®

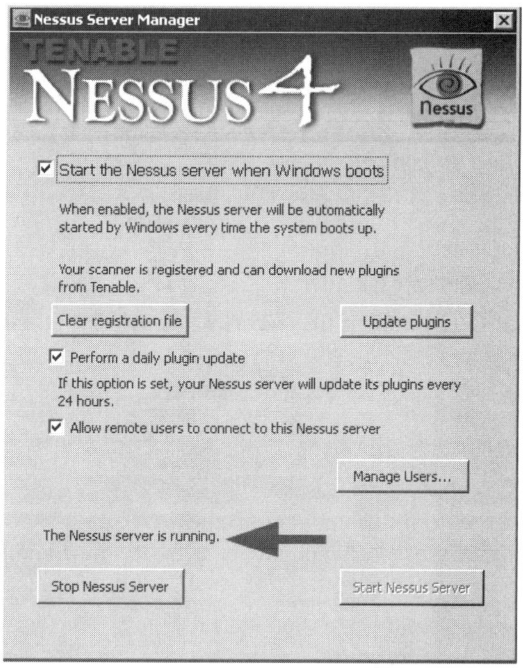

19. In the Nessus User Management dialog box, **click** on the **+ button** in the bottom left corner to open the **Add/Edit a user** dialog box.
20. **Type** the following login information:
    - User name: **student**
    - Password: **ISS316Security**
    - Password (again): **ISS316Security**
21. **Select** the **Administrator checkbox** to give this user administrative privileges.

22. **Click** the **Save** button to finish creating the new user account, and then click **Close**.

FIGURE 4.6

Add/Edit a user in Nessus Server Manager

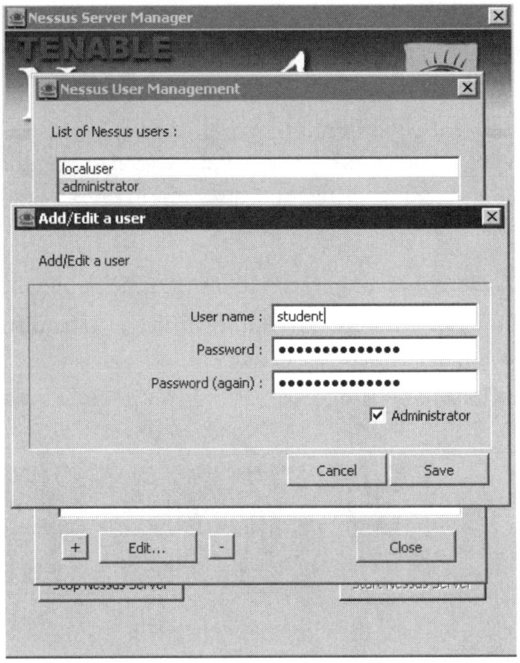

23. **Close** the **Nessus Server Manager window**.
24. **Double-click** the **Nessus Client icon** on the vWorkstation desktop to open the application in Internet Explorer browser.

Note:
The first time you connect to the Nessus Client, you will see a Web page that tells you that *There is a problem with this website's security certificate.* To proceed any further, you must click the Continue to this website (not recommended) link.

FIGURE 4.7

Certificate problem warning message

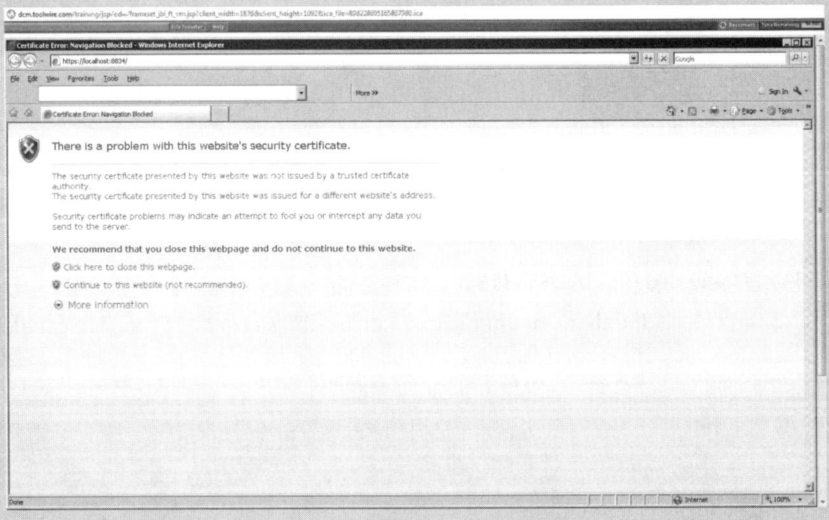

25. When the Nessus Client site appears, log in using the new user account you created in step 20:
    - User name: **student**
    - Password: **ISS316Security**

FIGURE 4.8

Log in to Nessus®

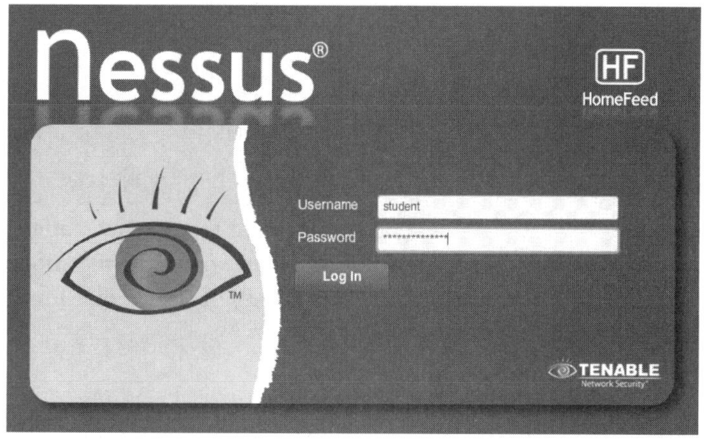

26. **Click** the **Log In button**.
27. **Click OK** to accept the Nessus HomeFeed Terms of Use and open the Nessus Client homepage.

FIGURE 4.9

Nessus Client homepage

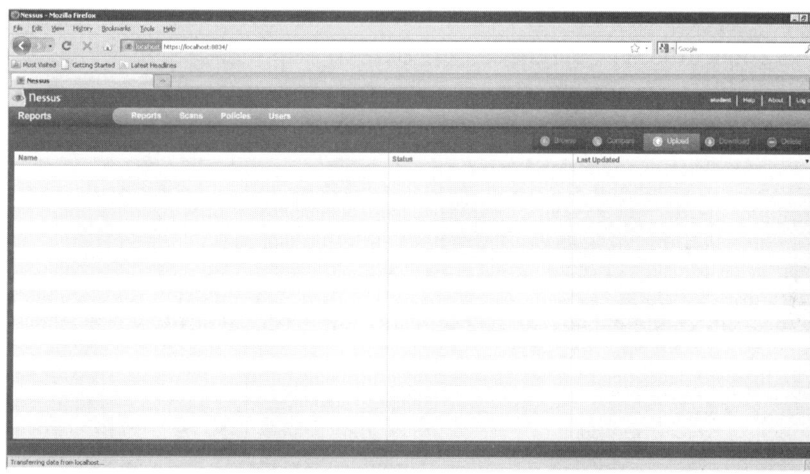

Note:

The next steps will create a custom security policy using the Nessus Client. This step, which configures the parameters for the scan, is required prior to conducting a vulnerability scan. The security policy includes:

- Parameters that control technical aspects of the scan, such as timeouts, number of hosts, type of port scanner, and more
- Credentials for local scans (e.g., Windows, SSH), authenticated Oracle Database scans, HTTP, FTP, POP, IMAP, or Kerberos-based authentication
- Granular family or plug-in-based scan specifications
- Database compliance policy checks, report verbosity, service detection scan settings, Unix compliance checks, and more

28. **Click** the **Policies tab** on the Nessus Client homepage.
29. **Click** the **Add button** to add a new policy.

    The Policies tab contains four configuration tabs: General, Credentials, Plugins, and Preferences. For most environments, the default settings do not need to be modified, but selecting each of these tabs will provide options for more granular control over the Nessus® scanner operation as described in the table.

TAB	CONFIGURABLE OPTIONS
General	Allows you to name your policy and define the scan-related operations.
Credentials	Allows you to configure the Nessus® scanner to use authentication credentials during scanning. By configuring credentials, it allows Nessus® to perform a wider variety of checks that result in more accurate scan results.
Plugins	Enables the user to choose specific security checks by plug-in family or individual checks.
Preferences	Displays further configuration items for the selected category. This is a dynamic list of configuration options that is dependent on the plug-in feed, audit policies, and additional functionality that the connected Nessus® scanner has access to.

30. In the **Name** box, **type Lab #4 Policy**.
31. **Click** the **TCP Scan checkbox** in the Port Scanners section of the screen to add that option to the selections already set on the General tab.
32. In the Scan section of the screen, **click** the following **checkboxes** to add these options:
    - **Save Knowledge Base**
    - **Log Scan Details to Server**
    - **Stop Host Scan on Disconnect**
    - **Designate Hosts by their DNS Name**
33. **Click** the **Next button** to accept the new settings for the **General tab** and display the **Credentials tab**.

FIGURE 4.10

Creating Lab #4 Policy

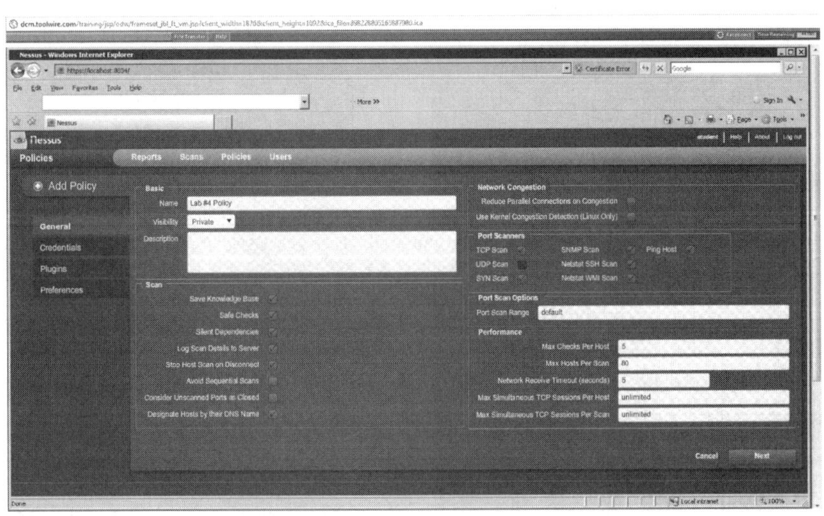

34. Explore the configuration options on the Credentials tab, but do not make any adjustments or change any fields. **Click Next.**
35. In the Families section of the Plugins tab, **double-click** the following **Families** to add these options to the Plugins window and **click Next** to open the Preferences tab:
    - **Databases**
    - **Default Unix Accounts**
    - **Ubuntu Local Security Checks**
    - **Web Servers**

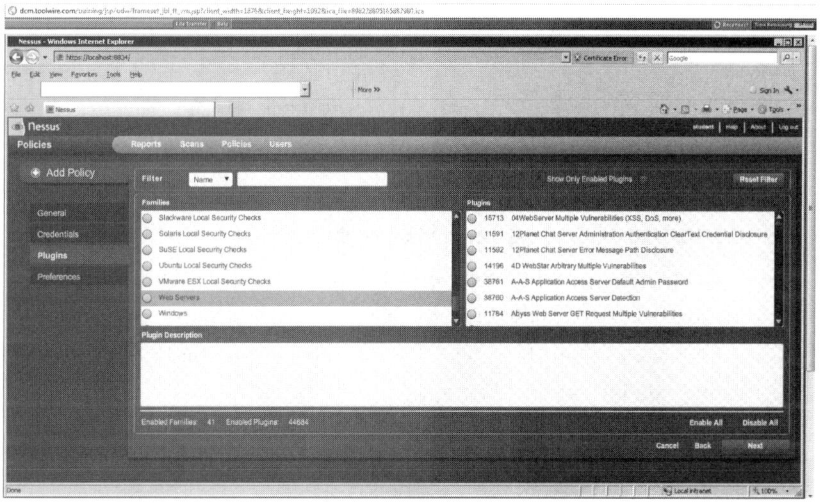

FIGURE 4.11

Selecting Plugins for the Lab #4 Policy

36. Save the **Lab #4 Policy** parameters by clicking **Submit** on the final screen.

    The newly created Lab #4 Policy now appears on the Policies page.

> **Note:**
> The next steps will identify Microsoft® Windows XP Professional Workstation and application vulnerabilities. You will first create a scan definition, then run the scan and examine any vulnerabilities found by the Nessus Client.

37. **Click** the **Scans tab** on the Nessus Client toolbar.

38. **Click** the **Add button** to add a new scan and use the information in the following steps to configure the information described in the table.

FIELD LABEL	CONFIGURABLE OPTIONS
Name	Sets the name that will be displayed in the Nessus® UI to identify the scan.
Type	Choose between Run Now (immediately execute the scan after submitting) or Template (save as a template for repeat scanning).
Policy	Select a previously created policy that the scan will use to set parameters controlling Nessus® server scanning behavior.
Scan Targets	Targets can be entered by single IP address (192.168.0.1), IP range (192.168.0.1-192.168.0.255), subnet with CIDR notation (192.168.0.0/24), or resolvable host (www.Nessus.org).
Targets File	A text file with a list of hosts can be imported by clicking on Browse and selecting a file from the local machine. Example host file formats and individual hosts include: • 192.168.0.100, 192.168.0.101, 192.168.0.102 • Host range: 192.168.0.100-192.168.0.102 • Host CIDR block: 192.168.0.1/24

39. In the **Name** box, **type Lab #4 Vulnerability Scan.**
40. In the **Type** box, **select Run Now** from the drop-down menu.
41. In the **Policy** box, **select Lab #4 Policy** from the drop-down menu.
42. In the **Scan Targets** box, **type IP address/24** using the IP address you recorded in step 9.
43. Leave the **Targets File** box empty.

FIGURE 4.12

Creating parameters for Lab #4 Vulnerability Scan

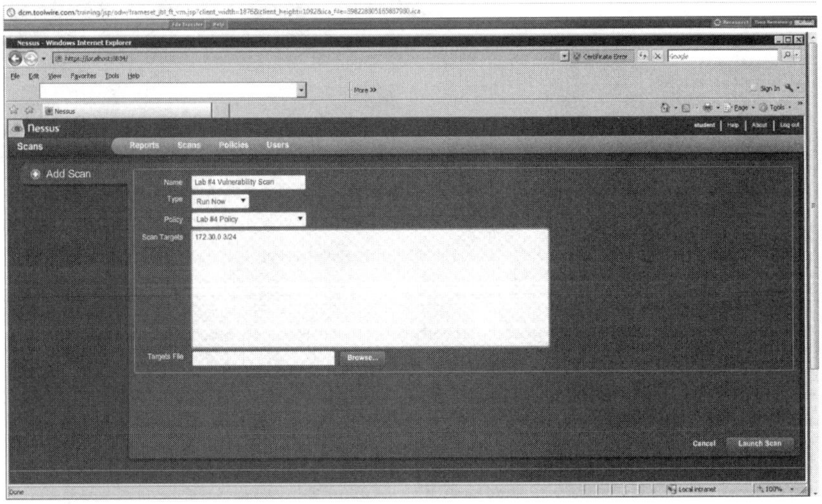

44. **Click** the **Launch Scan button** to start the scan.

The scan will begin immediately and a status bar, colored yellow, will indicate the progress of the scan. You can use the control buttons at the top of the Scans screen to Pause, Resume, or Stop the scan. Use the Browse button to see more detail about the progress of the scan for each target being scanned.

FIGURE 4.13

Lab #4 Nessus Scan progress bar

45. **Click** the **Reports tab** in the toolbar at the top to show the running and completed scans. The Reports screen acts as a central point for viewing, comparing, uploading, and downloading scan results.
46. **Double-click** the **Lab #4 Vulnerability Scan** line item to open the report for that scan.

The first screen you see is the summary screen, which gives an overview of hosts scanned and vulnerabilities discovered. Vulnerabilities are categorized according to severity: High, Medium, and Low. You can also access the scan report by first clicking on the report name and then clicking the Browse button.

FIGURE 4.14

Nessus® report summary

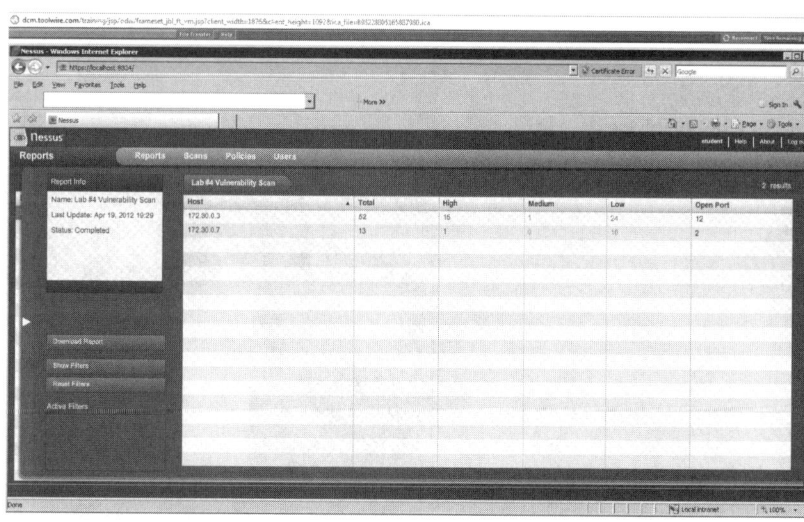

47. **Click** the **High column header** to sort the Hosts by vulnerability level. This will display the host with the greatest number of high-severity vulnerabilities at the top of the list.

Clicking a column header will toggle the displayed results either in descending order (greatest to least) or in ascending order (least to greatest). If you clicked the High column header and found your results displayed in ascending order, click the column header again to change the order and proceed to the next step.

48. **Double-click** the host at the top of the list (the one with the greatest number of high-severity vulnerabilities) to open the report's detail screen.

    Just below the Nessus® toolbar, on the Reports screen, you will see a "breadcrumb trail" of report pages. This trail is displayed as a series of clickable arrows.

FIGURE 4.15

"Breadcrumb trail" of Nessus® reports

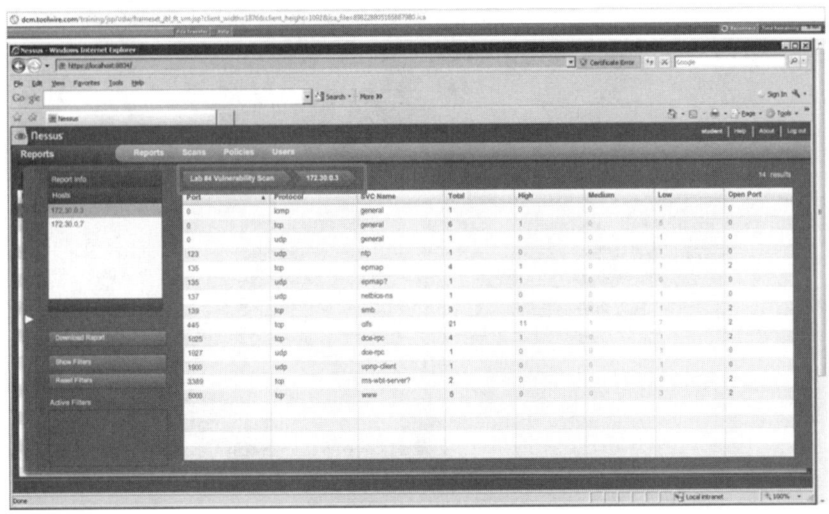

49. On the host detail screen, sort the port numbers by severity level by **clicking** the **High column header**.
50. **Double-click** the port number with the highest severity to see more information about the vulnerabilities on that port.
51. **Locate** the **MS08-067 vulnerability** and **double-click** to see the full details of the error finding, including a technical description, references, solution, detailed risk factor, and any relevant output. The details in the vulnerability Plugin ID provide overview, solution, risk factor, and CVE listing information.

FIGURE 4.16

Error description of the MS08-067 vulnerability

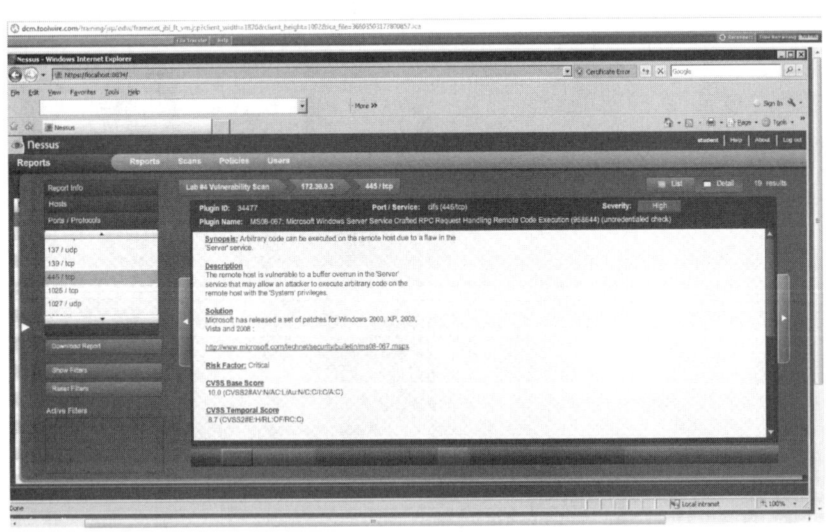

52. **Make a screen capture** of the error description and **paste** it into your text document. You may have to take multiple screen captures to display the entire output. You will need this information in a later step.

> **Note:**
> To capture the screen, **press** the **Ctrl** and **PrtSc** keys together, and then **use Ctrl + V** to paste the image into a Word or other word processor document.

53. **Click** the **Lab #4 Vulnerability Scan arrow** in the breadcrumb trail at the top of the report to return to the report summary homepage.
54. **Click** the **Download Report button** on the left-hand menu to save a copy of the report. You will need this file for the deliverables of this lab.
55. In the Download Report dialog box, **select HTML export** from the drop-down menu and **click Submit**.

FIGURE 4.17
Homepage of HTML export report, including list of hosts

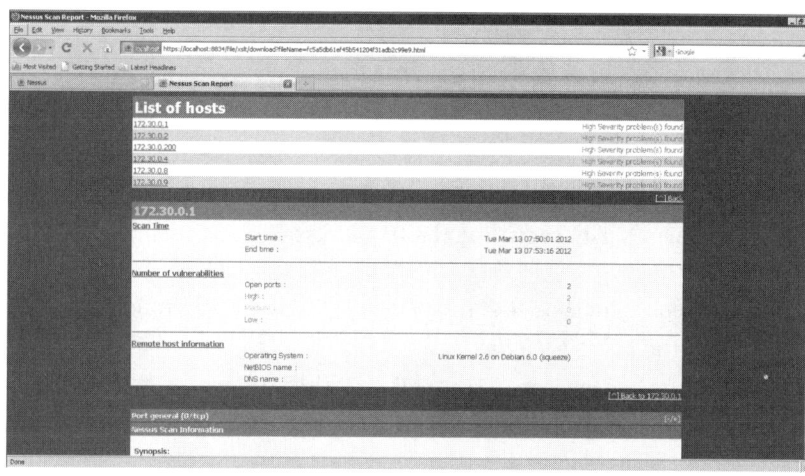

56. In the Internet Explorer toolbar, **click File > Save As**.
57. In the Save Webpage dialog box, **select Webpage, complete (*.htm,*.html)** in the Save as type box and **click Save** to save the report to the Security_Strategies folder (**My Computer > Local Disk (C:) > Security_Strategies**).
58. Use the **File Transfer button** on the vWorkstation desktop to transfer the document to your physical workstation and submit it to your instructor with the deliverables for this lab.
59. **Close** the **Nessus Scan Report window** to exit the report.
60. **Close** the **Internet Explorer browser window** to exit the Nessus Client.
61. **Close** the **Nessus Server Manager**.

> **Note:**
> The next steps will compromise and exploit a Microsoft® Windows XP Professional Workstation and a vulnerable application using the BackTrack4 Metasploit Framework.

62. In the ISSA_VM Server Farm_RDP window on the vWorkstation desktop, **double-click** the **BackTrack4 icon** to open that application.

63. **Log in** to the **BackTrack4 Framework** using the following security credentials:
    - Login: **root**
    - Password: **toor**

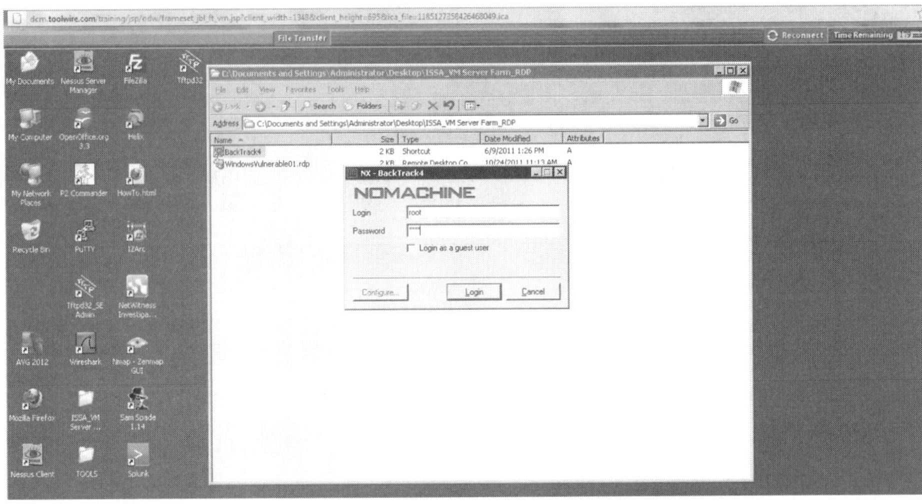

FIGURE 4.18
BackTrack4 login screen

64. **Click** the **Konsole Terminal Program icon** in the toolbar at the bottom of the window.
65. **Type ping IP address** (using the IP address you recorded in step 9) to verify that the WindowsVulnerable01 is accepting connections.

    The replies indicate that the WindowsVulnerable01 machine is accepting connections.
66. **Close** the **Konsole window**.
67. **Click** the **K menu icon** in the toolbar at the bottom of the window and **select Backtrack > Penetration > Metaspolit Exploitation Framework > Framework Version 3 > Msfweb**.

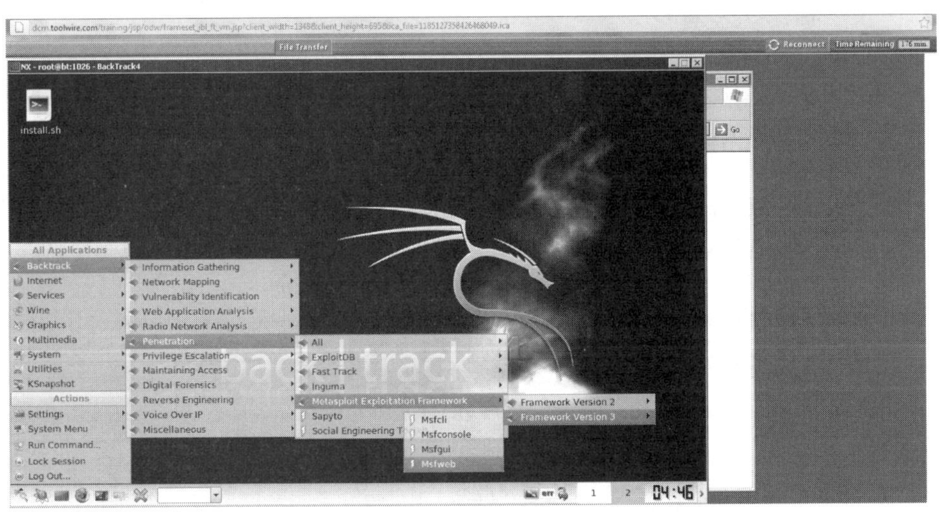

FIGURE 4.19
Opening the Metasploit Framework v3 Msfweb application

68. As the Msfweb tool loads, the shell displays a loopback IP address. **Record** the **loopback IP address** *(loopback address=_________________:55555)*. You will need this information in a later step.
69. **Click** the **Mozilla Firefox browser icon** in the toolbar at the bottom of the screen.

70. In the browser's address box, **type *loopback address*:55555** using the loopback address you recorded in step 68 and **press Enter**.

    The Web console will load with a system message at the bottom of the screen indicating that scripts are forbidden.

FIGURE 4.20

Metasploit Framework's Web console

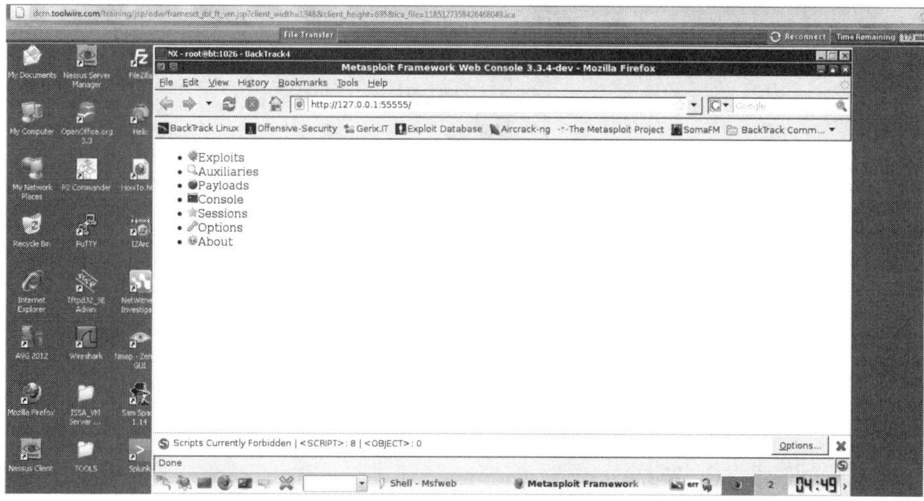

71. **Click** the **Options button** in the error message and **select Allow Scripts Globally (dangerous)** from the context menu.

FIGURE 4.21

Allowing scripts for the Metasploit Framework

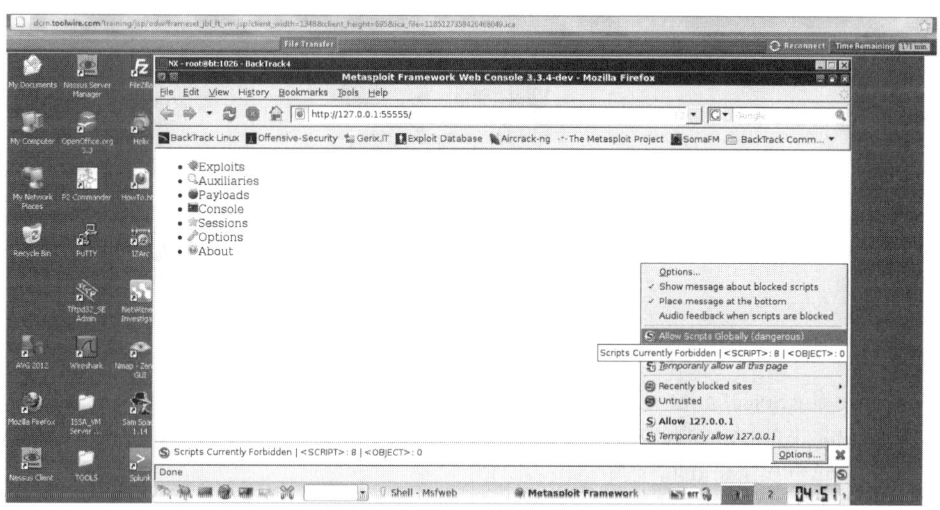

72. **Click OK** in the warning window to accept scripts and load Metasploit.
73. **Click** the **Exploits button** on the Metasploit toolbar to open Metasploit's Available Exploits search tool.

74. In the Available Exploits search box, **type MS08-067** (one of the vulnerabilities identified by the Nessus® scan) to review a description of the vulnerability.

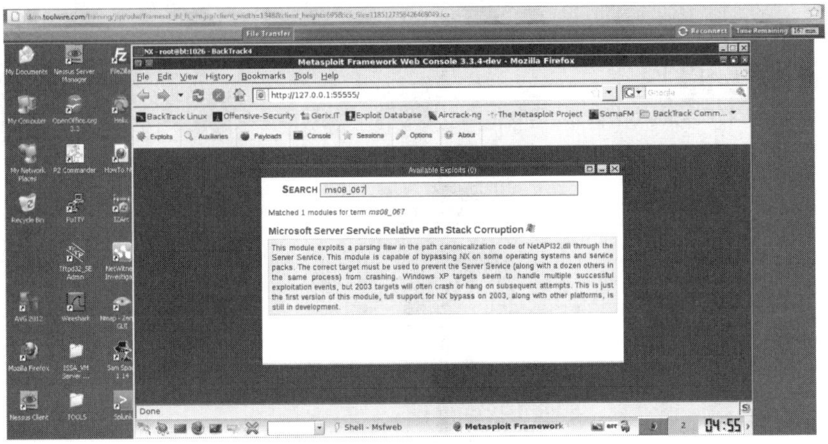

FIGURE 4.22

Metasploit's description of the MS08_067 vulnerability

75. **Double-click** the **Microsoft® Server Service Relative Path Stack Corruption link**.

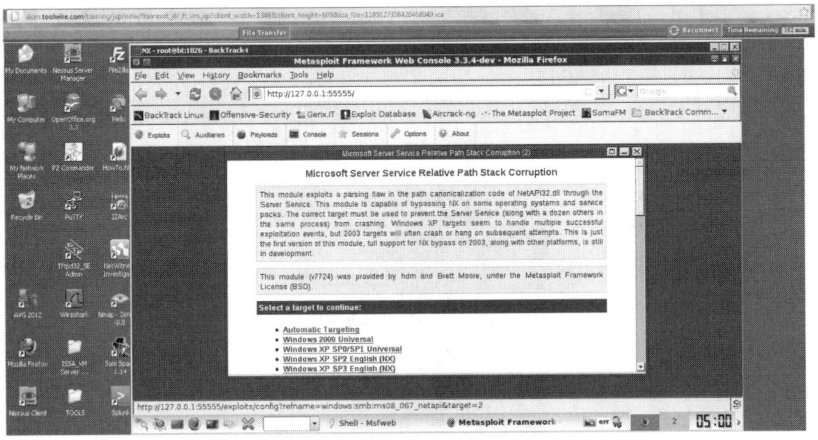

FIGURE 4.23

Microsoft® Server Service Relative Path Stack Corruption targets

76. In the Select a target to continue section of the page, **click** the **Windows XP SP0/SP1 Universal link**.

Metasploit displays the selected exploit (MS08-067), the selected target (Windows XP SP0/SP1 Universal), and a list of options.

77. **Click** the **generic/shell_bind_tcp link** to listen for a connection and spawn a command shell.

FIGURE 4.24

Selecting the generic/shell_bind_tcp exploit

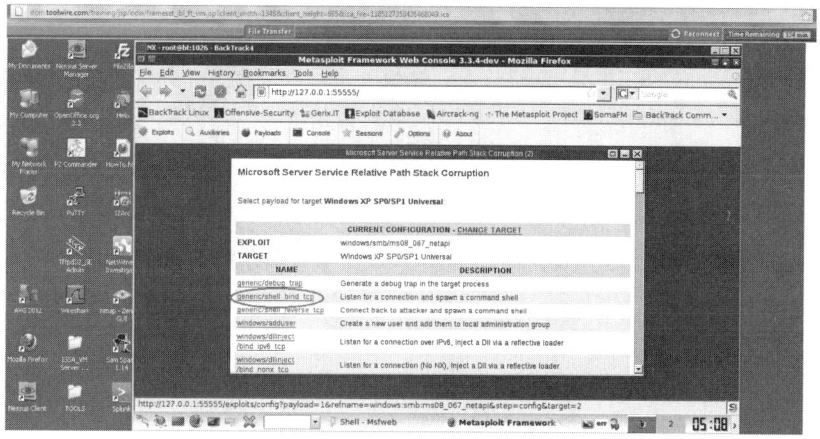

78. **Maximize** the **Microsoft® Server Service Relative Path Stack Corruption window** within the Metasploit application.
79. In the RHOST box, **type IP address**, using the IP address for the WindowsVulnerable01 machine that you recorded in step 9.

FIGURE 4.25

Launching the exploit

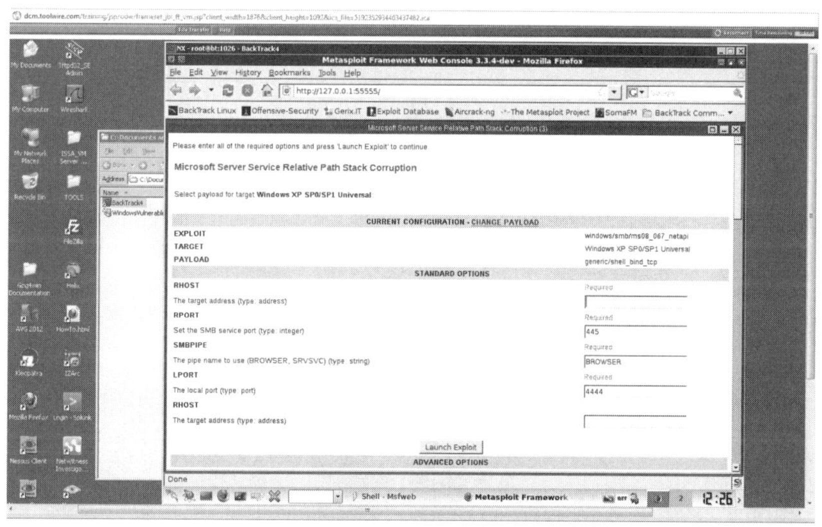

80. **Click** the **Launch Exploit button**.

    A new window pops up with a status message indicating that the test is running. When the test is complete, you should see a message indicating the success or failure of your attack. This process can take several minutes, but a successful hack will grant you full system administrator privileges to create additional users and change or manipulate files, including the ability to read, write, copy, and delete files.

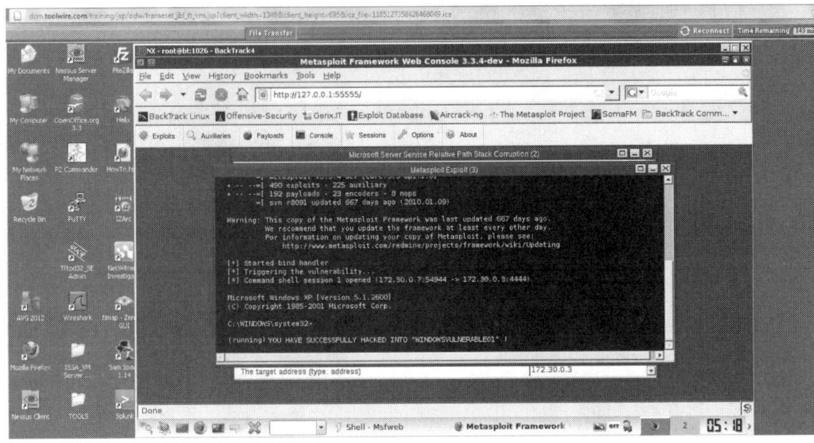

FIGURE 4.26

A successful hack into the WindowsVulnerable01 machine

81. **Make a screen capture** of the successful exploit and **paste** it into your text document.
82. **Close** the **BackTrack4 window**.
83. **Click Disconnect** when prompted to disconnect the session and return to the vWorkstation desktop.
84. **Close** the **ISSA_VM Server Farm_RDP folder**.

> **Note:**
> The next steps will remediate the vulnerability and eliminate the risk from exploitation by recommending security countermeasures.

85. **Review** the screen capture of the **vulnerability description for MS08-067** that you copied in step 52.
86. **Locate** the **hyperlink** in the portion of the screen that describes the solution.
87. From a workstation with Internet access, **open** an **Internet browser** and, in the browser's address bar, **type** the **hyperlink** you identified in step 86.

    The hyperlink will open a Microsoft® Security Bulletin describing the vulnerability and providing links to software patches that resolve the issue.

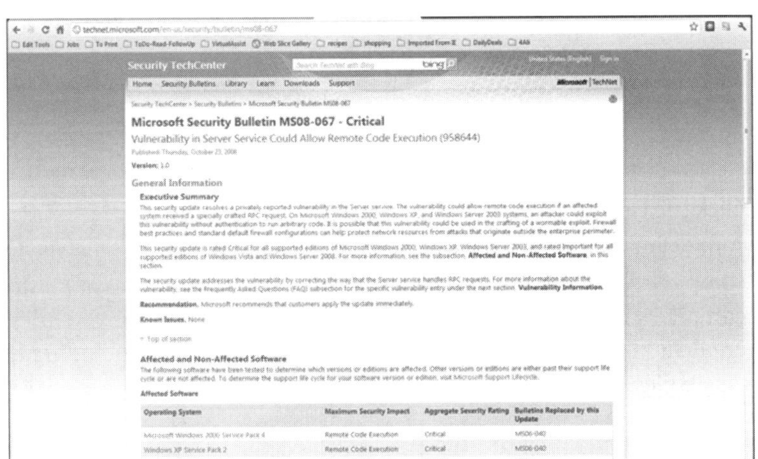

FIGURE 4.27

Microsoft® Security Bulletin for MS08-067

88. **Make a screen capture** of the Microsoft® Security Bulletin and **paste** it into your text document. You may have to take multiple screen captures to display the entire output.
89. **Identify** the **correct software patch** for the Windows version you selected in step 76 and follow the online instructions to **download** the **software patch** to your workstation. **Submit** this file to your instructor as a deliverable for this lab.
90. Use the **File Transfer button** to download the **text file** to your local computer and submit it as part of your deliverables.

Evaluation Criteria and Rubrics

The following are the evaluation criteria and rubrics for Lab #4 that the students must perform:

1. Was the student able to demonstrate reconnaissance and probing using Zenmap GUI to identify live hosts and their common ports, services, and applications running in production? – [**20%**]
2. Was the student able to perform a vulnerability scan on the identified IP host and Microsoft® workstations using Nessus®? – [**20%**]
3. Was the student able to identify software vulnerabilities from the vulnerability assessment scan report and the CVE listing for this vulnerability? – [**20%**]
4. Was the student able to exploit the known software vulnerability using the BackTrack4 Live CD tool and Metasploit Framework to attack a known Microsoft® vulnerable workstation? – [**20%**]
5. Was the student able to recommend specific security countermeasures for the vulnerable Microsoft® workstation based on the results of the vulnerability assessment findings and system compromise? – [**20%**]

LAB #4 – ASSESSMENT WORKSHEET

Compromise and Exploit a Vulnerable Microsoft® Workstation

Course Name and Number: ___

Student Name: ___

Instructor Name: ___

Lab Due Date: ___

Overview

In this lab, you explored all five phases of hacking using Zenmap GUI for Nmap, Nessus®, BackTrack4, and the Metasploit Framework application.

Lab Assessment Questions & Answers

1. What are the five steps of a hacking attack?

2. During the reconnaissance step of the attack, describe what task Zenmap GUI performs to do passive OS fingerprinting.

3. What step in the ethical hacking attack process uses Zenmap GUI?

4. What step in the hacking attack process identifies known vulnerabilities and exploits?

5. During the scanning step of the hacking attack process, you identified known software vulnerabilities in a Windows XP Professional Workstation. List the name and number of the critical Microsoft® vulnerabilities identified. What is vulnerability "MS08-067"?

6. Which tool and application were used to exploit the identified vulnerability on the targeted Microsoft® Windows 2003 server?

7. If you were a member of a security penetration testing team, and you identified vulnerabilities and exploits, should you obtain written permission from the owners prior to compromising and exploiting the known vulnerability?

8. The most important step in the five-step ethical hacking process is the last step in which the security practitioner must remediate the vulnerability and eliminate the exploit. What is the name and number of the Microsoft® Security Bulletin?

____

____

____

____

9. What is the name of the Microsoft® Windows XP Security Patch needed to remediate this software vulnerability and exploit?

____

____

____

____

Perform a Website and Database Attack by Exploiting Identified Vulnerabilities

LAB 5

Introduction

In this lab, you will verify and perform a cross-site scripting (XSS) exploit and an SQL injection attack on the test bed Web application and Web server using the Damn Vulnerable Web Application (DVWA) found on the TargetUbuntu01 Linux VM server. You will first identify the IP target host, identify known vulnerabilities and exploits, and then attack the Web application and Web server using a Web browser and some simple command strings.

Learning Objectives

Upon completing this lab, you will be able to:

- Identify Web application and Web server backend database vulnerabilities as viable attack vectors
- Develop an attack plan to compromise and exploit a website using cross-site scripting (XSS) against sample vulnerable Web applications
- Conduct a manual cross-site scripting (XSS) attack against sample vulnerable Web applications
- Perform SQL injection attacks against sample vulnerable Web applications with e-commerce data entry fields
- Mitigate known Web application and Web server vulnerabilities with security countermeasures to eliminate risk from compromise and exploitation

TOOLS AND SOFTWARE

NAME	MORE INFORMATION
Damn Vulnerable Web Application (DVWA)	http://www.dvwa.co.uk

Deliverables

Upon completion of this lab, you are required to provide the following deliverables to your instructor:

1. A written report that includes a summary of the following items:
    a. Enumeration: Identification of the exploits;
    b. Compromise and exploit:
        i. Screen capture of the cross-site scripting (XSS) attack;
        ii. Screen capture of the SQL injection attack;
        iii. Screen capture of the contents of the testing1.txt file;
    c. Remediation: Recommendations for mitigation of these vulnerabilities;
2. Lab Assessment Questions & Answers for Lab #5.

Hands-On Steps

1. This lab begins at the student landing vWorkstation virtual machine desktop of the VSCL, as shown here.

FIGURE 5.1

"Student Landing" VSCL workstation

> **Note:**
> The next steps access the Damn Vulnerable Web Application (DVWA) using an Internet browser. You will change the security level of DVWA to low so that you will be able to perform the steps in the rest of the lab.

2. **Double-click** the **Mozilla Firefox icon** on the desktop to open the Firefox browser.

   You can access the DVWA tool using any Internet browser, but the steps in this lab will use the Firefox browser.

3. **Type http://172.30.0.4/dvwa** in the browser's address box and **press Enter**.

FIGURE 5.2

DVWA login screen

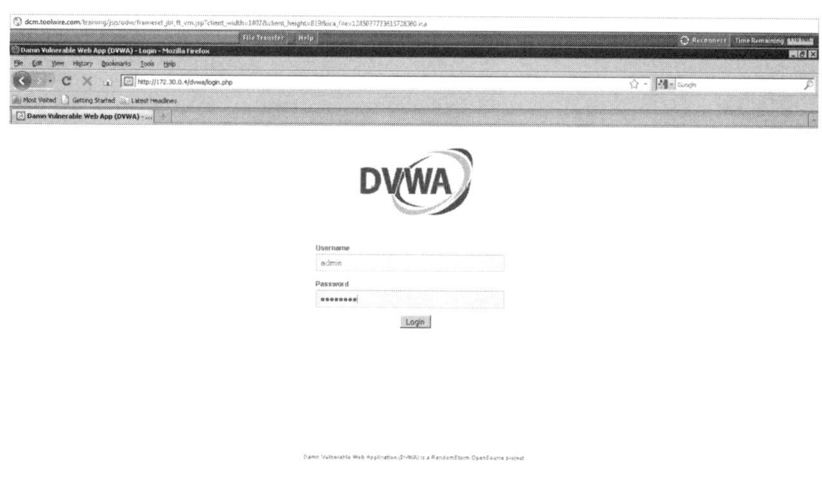

4. **Log in** to the application with the following credentials and **click Login** to continue:
   - Username: **admin**
   - Password: **password**
5. On the DVWA Welcome screen, **click** the **DVWA Security button**.
6. **Select low** from the Script Security drop-down menu. **Click Submit** to change the security level.

FIGURE 5.3

Changing the script security level in DVWA

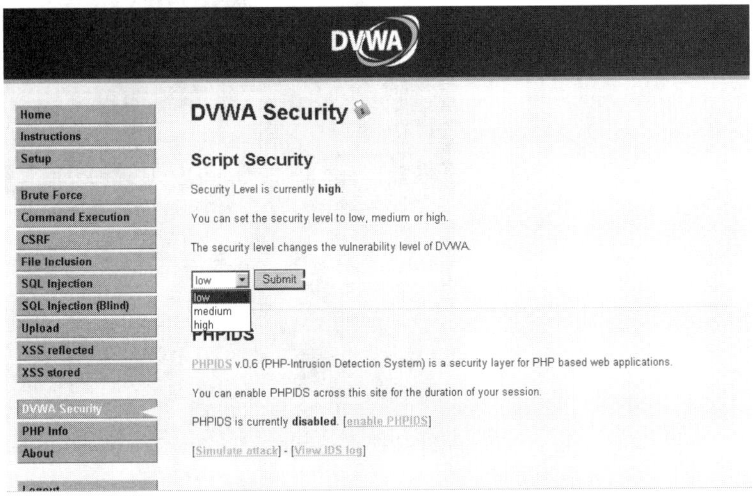

> **Note:**
> The next steps use the DVWA tool to perform an attack by exploiting a cross-site scripting (XSS) vulnerability. The goal of an XSS attack is usually to gain administrator or some other elevated level of user privileges.

7. **Click** the **XSS reflected button** in the DVWA navigation menu.

   XSS vulnerabilities are generally found in Web forms that send and retrieve data to databases via HTML.
8. In the What's your name? box, **type Simon** and **click Submit**.

   The Web form will take the name you entered and repeat it back to you in a friendly welcome.

FIGURE 5.4

Expected output from XSS test

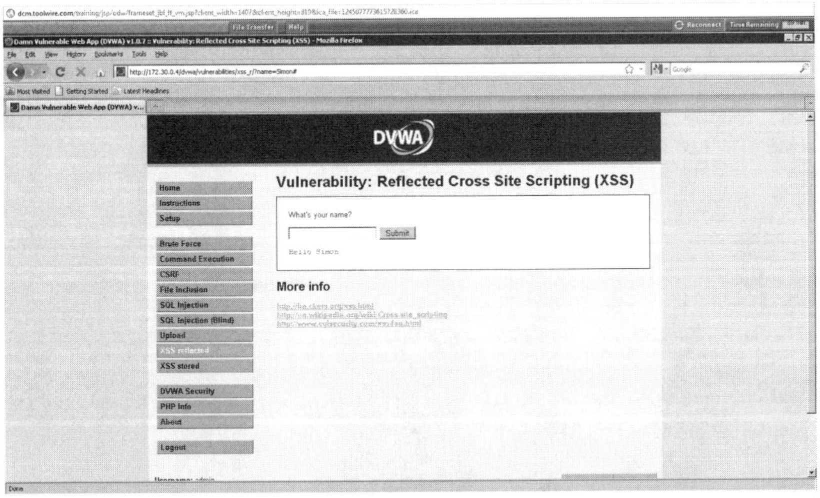

9. In the What's your name? box, **type <this is a test>** and **click Submit**.

   The Web form cannot handle the unexpected data and fails to return the expected outcome. You have uncovered a vulnerability in this form.

FIGURE 5.5

Testing the XSS reflected vulnerability

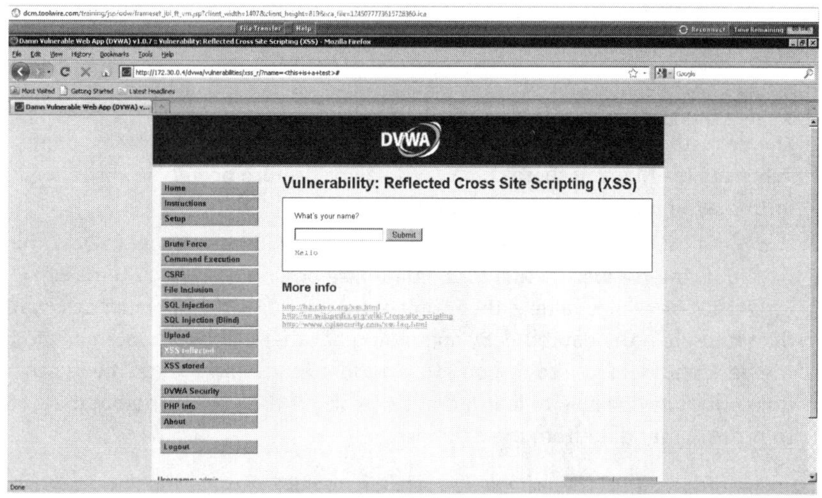

10. In the What's your name? box, **type <script>alert('vuln');</script> Hello!** and **click Submit**.

    The Web form processed the script and returned a popup alert window.

FIGURE 5.6

Alert window processed by the Web form

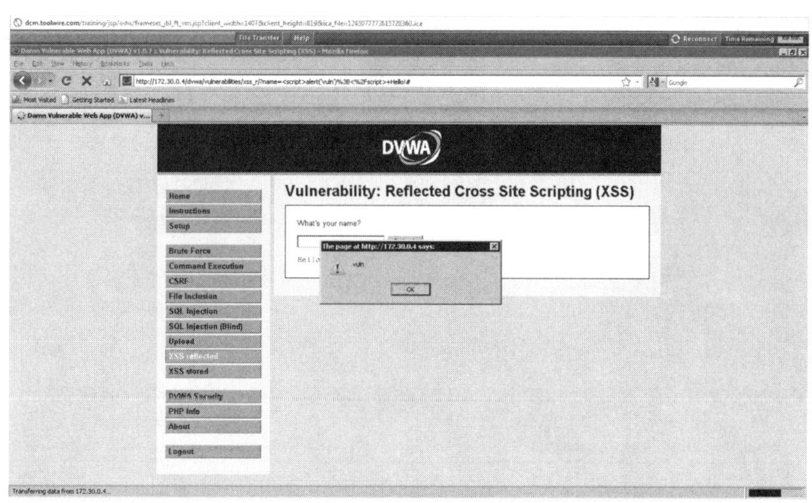

11. **Click OK** to close the alert window.

12. **Make a screen capture** showing the exposed vulnerability and **paste** it into a new text document.

> **Note:**
> To capture the screen, **press** the **Ctrl** and **PrtSc** keys together, and then use **Ctrl + V** to paste the image into a Word or other word processor document.

> **Note:**
> The next steps will insert a series of SQL statements into a Web form to find and then exploit a SQL injection vulnerability. Many of these commands will not return any errors. Experienced hackers will continue probing until they find the data they were seeking.
>
> In general, SQL injection is accomplished by appending some valid SQL command to the input that is being passed through a web form into the database behind it. Most of the time when you provide a value in a field on a web form, that value is then compared, through an embedded SQL statement on the web server side, to data housed in the database. By appending another valid SQL statement to that value, you can attempt to get the back end database to respond to two queries instead of one. If you can also get it to respond to a second query, you may be able to learn something about the underlying database structure, or even get the web form to return other data from the database.

13. **Click** the **SQL Injection button** in the DVWA navigation menu.

    Poorly designed and secured Web forms can be exploited to output passwords, credit card information, and other data.

14 In the User ID box, **type O'Malley** and **click Submit**.

    The Web form was unable to handle the special character of an apostrophe. Often, programmers forget to include script handling for special characters in data input forms. This type of error can make an application vulnerable to SQL injection.

FIGURE 5.7

SQL error

15. **Click** the **browser's Back button** to return to the SQL Injection form in DVWA.

16. In the User ID box, **type a' OR 'x'='x';#** and **click Submit**.

    This script will return the first and last names of everyone in the application's database.

FIGURE 5.8

Results from the SQL injection test

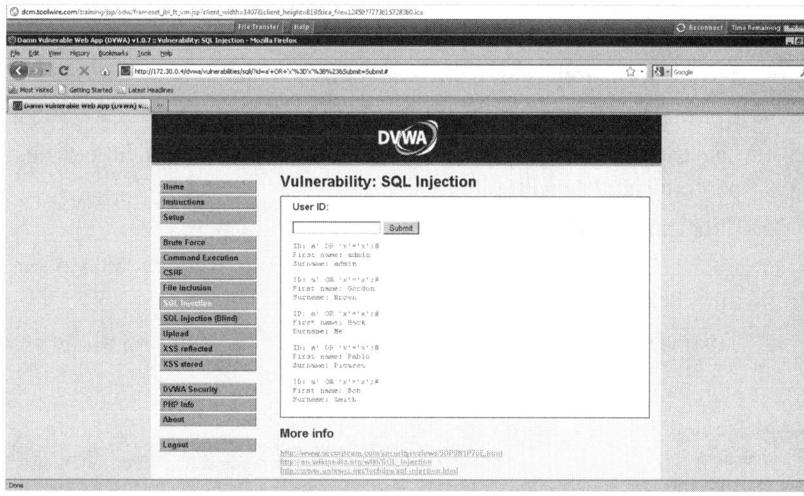

17. In the User ID box, **type a' ORDER BY 1;#** and **click Submit**.

    Review the output. If there is no error, indicating an SQL injection vulnerability, proceed to the next step. If you see an error statement, **click** the **browser's Back button** and proceed to step 19.

18. In the User ID box, **type a' ORDER BY 2;#** and **click Submit**.

    Review the output. If there is no error, indicating an SQL injection vulnerability, proceed to the next step. If you see an error statement, **click** the **browser's Back button** and proceed to step 19.

19. In the User ID box, **type a' ORDER BY 3;#** and **click Submit**.

    Review the output. If there is no error, indicating an SQL injection vulnerability, proceed to the next step. If you see an error statement, **click** the **browser's Back button** and proceed to step 19.

20. In the User ID box, **type a' OR firstname IS NULL;#** and **click Submit**.

    The error message indicates that the field name is spelled wrong.

FIGURE 5.9

Results from the "firstname" test

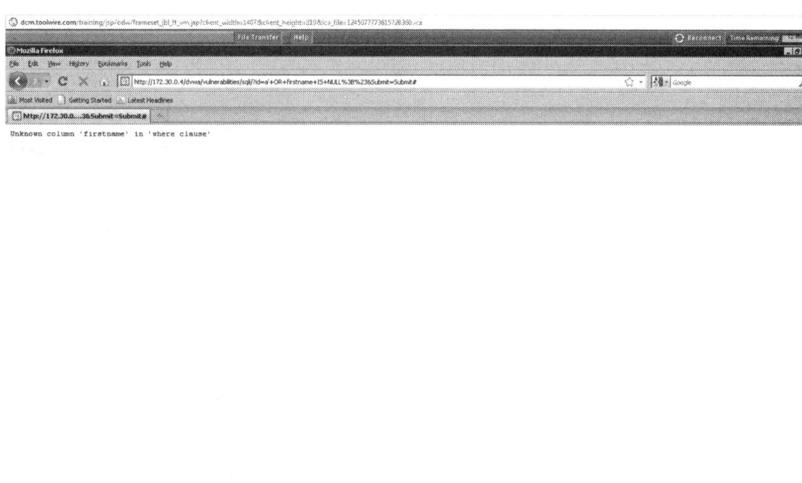

21. **Click** the **browser's Back button**.
22. In the User ID box, **type a' OR first_name IS NULL;#** and **click Submit** to try another common spelling for the name of this field.

    The lack of an error message indicates that the field name is now spelled correctly.
23. In the User ID box, **type a' OR database() LIKE 'DB';#** and **click Submit**.

    This script searches for a possible hit on the database's characters. Make note of any results you see.
24. In the User ID box, **type a' OR database() LIKE 'd%';#** and **click Submit**.

    Like the previous script, this one searches for a possible hit on the database's characters, but the percent sign (%) will split the fields.
25. **Click** the **browser's Back button**.
26. In the User ID box, **type a' UNION SELECT table_schema, table_name FROM information_Schema.tables;#** and **click Submit**.

    This script will return all of the table and column names in the database.

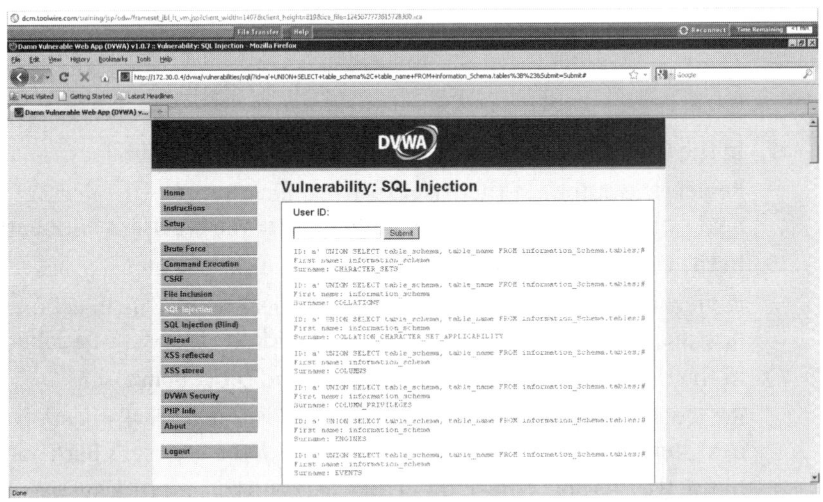

FIGURE 5.10

Results from the "table_schema, table_name" test

27. In the User ID box, **type a' UNION ALL SELECT 1, @@version;#** and **click Submit**.

    This script will return information about the version of SQL being used on the server.

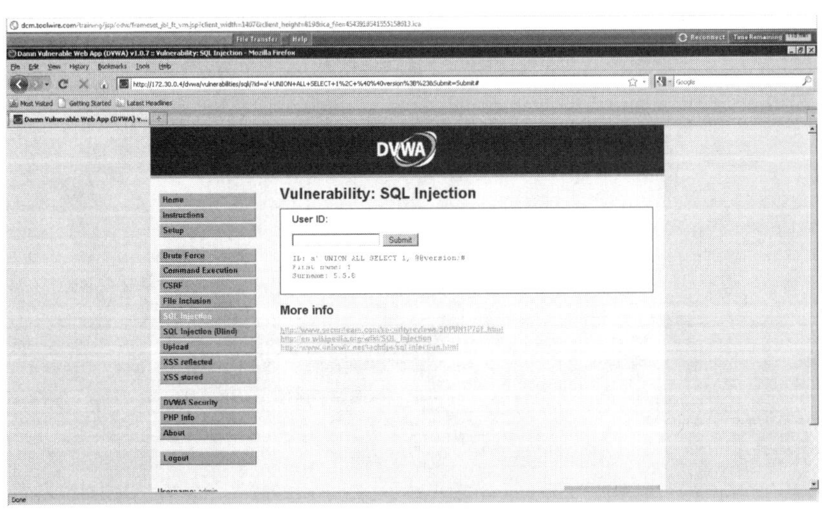

FIGURE 5.11

Results from the "@@version" test

28. In the User ID box, **type a' UNION ALL SELECT system_user(), user();#** and **click Submit.**

    This script will return information about the user name that you are using as you make queries on the server.

29. In the User ID box, **type a' UNION ALL SELECT user, password FROM mysql.user;# priv;# '** and **click Submit.**

    This script will give you a hash for the user to the backend database.

30. **Make a screen capture** showing the hash information and **paste** it into your text document.
31. In the User ID box, **type 'UNION SELECT 'test', '123' INTO OUTFILE 'testing1.txt** and **click Submit.**

    The DVWA application will display an error message, but this script should insert the phrases *test* and *123* into a new file called testing1.txt.

FIGURE 5.12

Writing the testing1.txt file

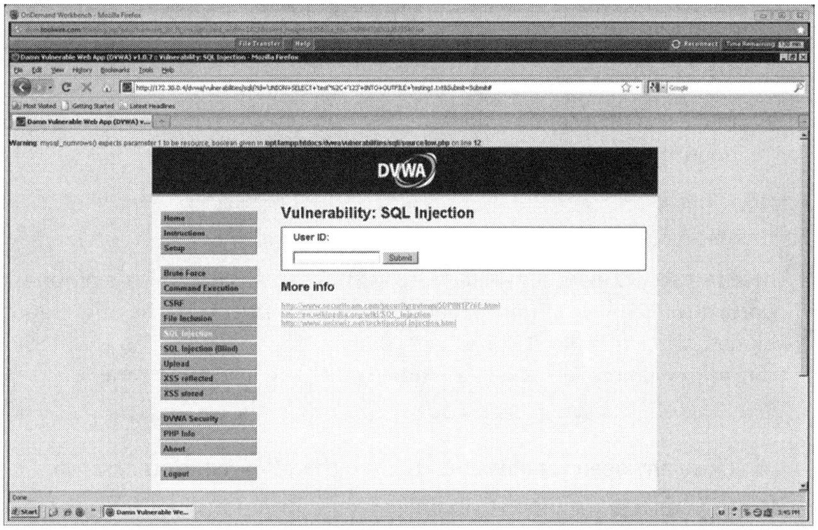

> **Note:**
> The next steps will verify that you have created the testing1.txt file on the TargetUbuntu01 server which is hosting the DVWA application.

32. **Minimize** the **Firefox browser** to return to the vWorkstation desktop.
33. **Double-click** the **ISSA_VM Server Farm_RDP icon** on the desktop. This folder contains links to the virtual servers in this environment.
34. **Double-click** the **TargetUbuntu01 file** to open the server.
35. **Log in** to the **TargetUbuntu01** server with the following credentials:
    - User name: **student**
    - Password: **ISS316Security**
36. **Click Applications > Accessories > Terminal** to open a terminal emulator and access the command prompt.
37. At the command prompt, **type sudo cat /opt/lampp/var/mysql/dvwa/testing1.txt** and **press Enter**.
38. When prompted for a password, **type ISS316Security** and **press Enter** to display the contents of the testing1.txt file that you created.

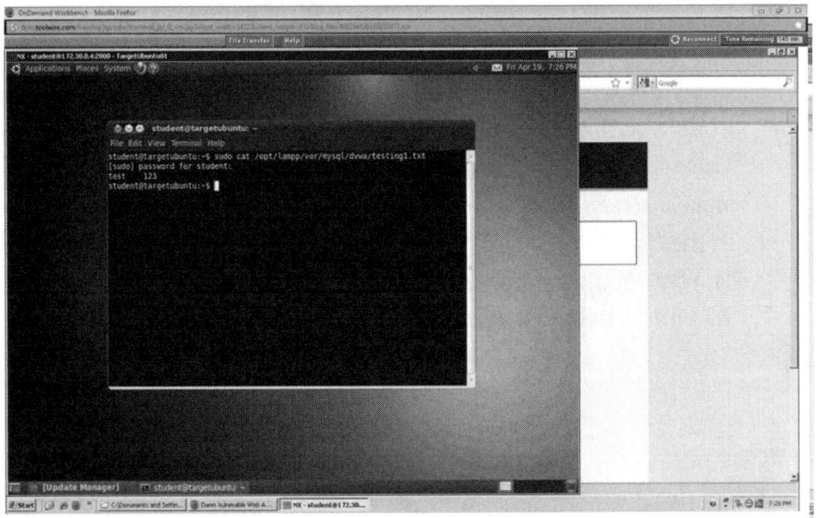

FIGURE 5.13

Viewing the contents of the testing1.txt file

39. **Make a screen capture** showing the contents of the testing1.txt file and **paste** it into your text document.

> **Note:**
> These test scripts were all typed in cleartext. Often hackers will use hexadecimal character strings instead of cleartext to make the scripts harder to detect. Together with the information you gathered in earlier tests, the ability to write to a file indicates that you have found a user with elevated permissions, user IDs, passwords, table and column information– –in other words, an injectable database.

40. **Close any open windows** to return to the vWorkstation desktop.
41. In your text document, organize your content into a summary of your findings, assessment, and recommendations report that includes:
    - Enumeration: Identify the exploit—what did you find?
    - Compromise and exploit: What were you able to do?
        - o Screen capture and description of the cross-site scripting attack—what did you compromise?
        - o Screen capture and description of the SQL injection attack—what did you extract?
        - o Screen capture of the testing1.txt file—what does this tell you about the exposed vulnerabilities?
    - Remediation: What security countermeasures do you recommend to mitigate the risk from compromise and exploitation?
42. Use the **File Transfer button** to download the **text document** to your local computer, **add** the rest of the requirements for this written report, and **submit** it as part of your deliverables for this lab.

Evaluation Criteria and Rubrics

The following are the evaluation criteria and rubrics for Lab #5 that students must perform:

1. Was the student able to identify Web application and Web server backend database vulnerabilities as viable attack vectors? – [**20%**]
2. Was the student able to develop an attack plan to compromise and exploit a website using cross-site scripting (XSS) against sample vulnerable Web applications? – [**20%**]
3. Was the student able to perform a manual cross-site scripting (XSS) attack against sample vulnerable Web applications? – [**20%**]
4. Was the student able to perform SQL injection attacks against sample vulnerable Web applications with e-commerce data entry fields? – [**20%**]
5. Was the student able to mitigate known Web application and Web server vulnerabilities with security countermeasures to eliminate risk from compromise and exploitation? – [**20%**]

LAB #5 – ASSESSMENT WORKSHEET

Perform a Website and Database Attack by Exploiting Identified Vulnerabilities

Course Name and Number: ______________________

Student Name: ______________________

Instructor Name: ______________________

Lab Due Date: ______________________

Overview

In this lab, you verified and performed a cross-site scripting (XSS) exploit and an SQL injection attack on the test bed Web application and Web server using the Damn Vulnerable Web Application (DVWA) found on the TargetUbuntu01 Linux VM server. You first identified the IP target host, identified known vulnerabilities and exploits, and then attacked the Web application and Web server using a Web browser and some simple command strings.

Lab Assessment Questions & Answers

1. Why is it critical to perform a penetration test on a Web application and a Web server prior to production implementation?

____

____

____

____

2. What is a cross-site scripting attack? Explain in your own words.

____

____

____

____

3. What is a reflective cross-site scripting attack?

4. Based on the tests you performed in this lab, which Web application attack is more likely to extract privacy data elements out of a database?

5. If you can monitor when SQL injections are performed on an SQL database, what would you recommend as a security countermeasure to monitor your production SQL databases?

6. Given that Apache and Internet Information Services (IIS) are the two most popular Web application servers for Linux and Microsoft® Windows platforms, what would you do to identify known software vulnerabilities and exploits?

7. What can you do to ensure that your organization incorporates penetration testing and Web application testing as part of its implementation procedures?

8. What is the purpose of setting the DVWA security level to low before beginning the remaining lab steps?

9. As an ethical hacker, once you've determined that a database is injectable, what should you do with that information?

Identify and Mitigate Malware and Malicious Software on a Windows Server

LAB 6

Introduction

In this lab, you will use AVG Business Edition 2012, an antivirus and anti-malware software tool, to identify the viruses, Trojans, or malware and malicious software found on a compromised system. Once the malware and malicious software is found and eliminated, you will craft a summary of findings report describing the problems and your recommendations for remediation.

Learning Objectives

Upon completing this lab, you will be able to:

- Identify malware and other malicious software on a Windows desktop using AVG antivirus and anti-malware tools
- Quarantine malware and other malicious software using antivirus and anti-malware for further investigation and removal
- Detect a hidden virus embedded in a PDF document with immediate quarantining by an AVG antivirus and anti-malware software tool
- Use AVG antivirus and anti-malware software tools to quarantine malware and malicious software in a Virus Vault for inspection and removal
- Draft a written report identifying what malware and malicious software was found and what remediation steps are needed to mitigate

TOOLS AND SOFTWARE

NAME	MORE INFORMATION
AVG	http://free.avg.com/us-en/homepage
IZarc Archiver	http://www.izarc.org/

Deliverables

Upon completion of this lab, you are required to provide the following deliverables to your instructor:

1. A summary of findings document that contains each of the following items:
   a. A screen capture of the AVG Virus Vault displaying the items found by the AVG scan;
   b. A screen capture showing any AVG alerts related to the prodrev.zip file;
   c. A screen capture of the AVG Virus Vault displaying any quarantined files;
   d. Recommended remediations for the malware and malicious software identified in this lab;
2. Lab Assessment Questions & Answers for Lab #6.

Hands-On Steps

1. This lab begins at the student landing vWorkstation virtual machine desktop of the VSCL, as shown here.

FIGURE 6.1

"Student Landing" VSCL workstation

> **Note:**
> The next steps use AVG to run a virus scan to identify and quarantine malware or malicious software on a Microsoft® Windows machine.

2. **Double-click** the **My Computer icon** on the desktop.
3. **Double-click** the **Local Disk (C:) icon** in the My Computer window.
4. **Double-click** the **Security_Strategies folder**.
5. **Double-click** the **ISSA_TOOLS folder**.
6. **Verify** that the **prodrev.zip file** appears in the folder. This encrypted zip file will be used later in the lab.

FIGURE 6.2

Locating the prodrev. zip file

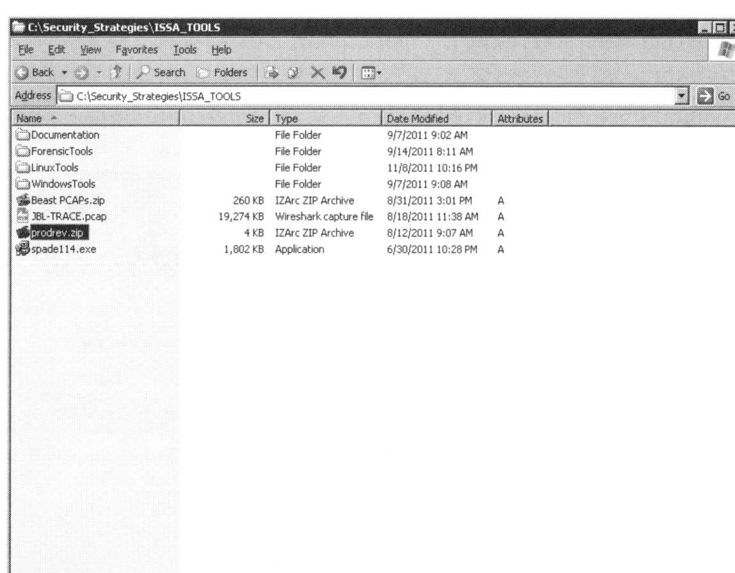

7. **Minimize** the **ISSA_TOOLS folder**.
8. **Double-click** the **AVG 2012 icon** on the desktop to start the antivirus application.
9. **Click** the **Update Now button** from the application's navigation bar.

   This computer does not have direct access to the Internet so selecting this option will have no effect in the lab and you will see a warning message in the applications header area throughout this part of the lab. However, this is an important step in performing a virus scan outside of the lab so it is included here.
10. **Click** the **Overview button** from the application's navigation bar.

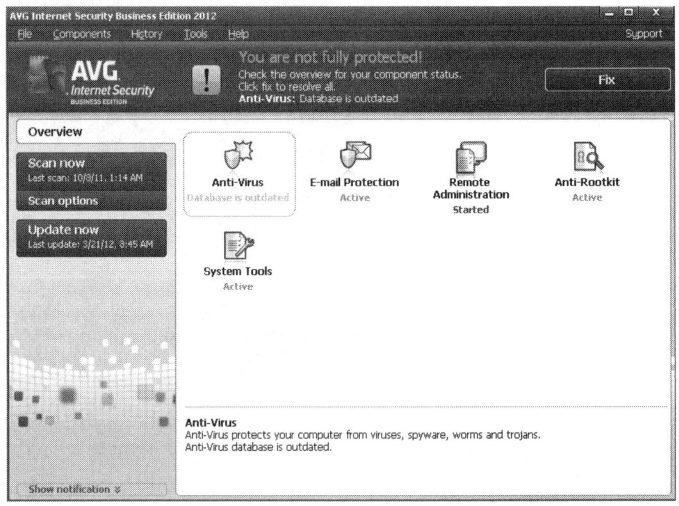

FIGURE 6.3

The AVG 2012 application window

11. **Click** the **Anti-Virus icon** on the AVG Overview page and review the features displayed on the resulting page. **Click** the **Cancel button** to return to the Overview page.
12. **Repeat step 11** for each of the remaining items on this page:
    - **E-mail Protection**
    - **Remote Administration**
    - **Anti-Rootkit**
    - **System Tools**
13. **Click** the **Scan now button** in the navigation bar.

    The default scan is a whole computer scan which should be indicated by a green arrow beneath the Scan option button in the navigation bar. This scan will take several minutes. Do not touch any keys until the scan is finished.

    When the scan is completed, AVG will display a summary of the threats that it identified and removed.

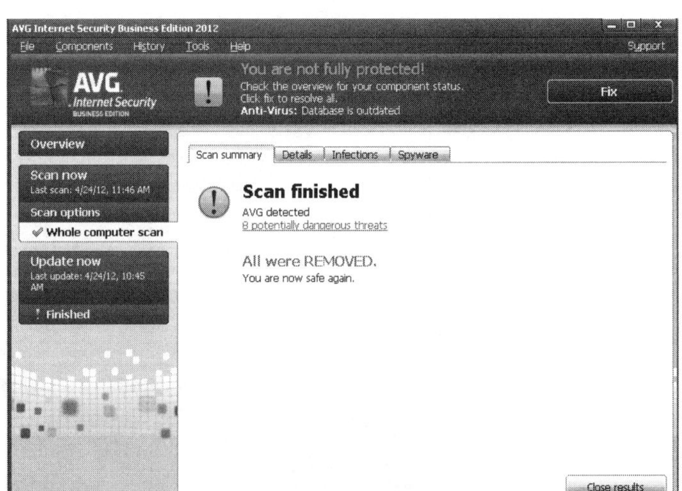

FIGURE 6.4

Scan summary for completed scan

14. In a new text document, **record** the **number of threats** identified by the scan.
15. **Click** the **Details tab** to see more specifics about the types of threats AVG identified.

FIGURE 6.5

Detailed summary of identified threats

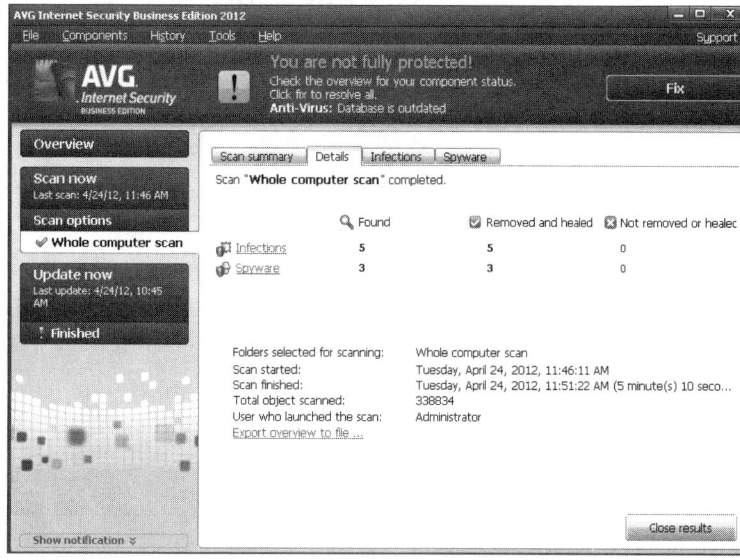

16. **Click** the **Infections tab** to see the specific infections found in this scan.

FIGURE 6.6

Infections identified in this scan

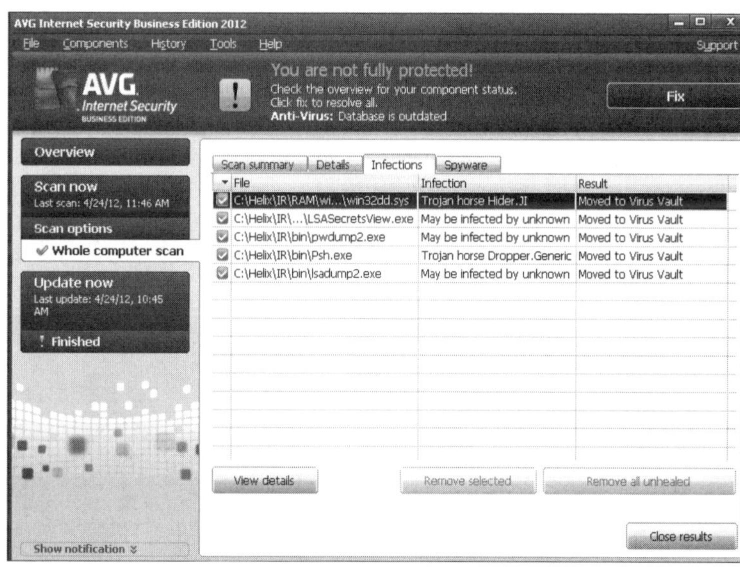

17. **Click** the first identified **infection**, and then **click** the **View details button** at the bottom of the window to get more information about it.
18. From a workstation with an Internet connection, **research** the **infection** found on this screen and the possible remediation steps. **Document your findings** in your text document.
19. **Click** the **Close button** to return to the Infections tab.
20. **Repeat** steps 17 through 19 for each of the threats identified by AVG.

21. **Click** the **Spyware tab** to see the specific spyware found in this scan.

FIGURE 6.7

Spyware and other malicious software identified in this scan

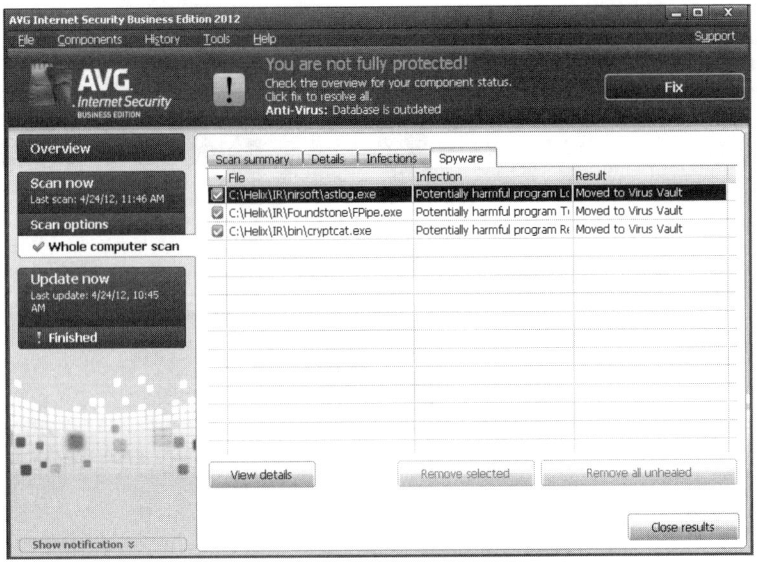

22. **Click** the first identified **spyware**, and then **click** the **View details button** at the bottom of the window to get more information about it.
23. From a workstation with an Internet connection, **research** the **spyware** found on this screen and the possible remediation steps. **Document your findings** in your text document.
24. **Click** the **Close button** to return to the Spyware tab.
25. **Repeat** steps 22 through 24 for each of the threats identified by AVG.
26. **Select History > Virus Vault** from the AVG menu to confirm that all malicious software and malware identified by the scan is properly quarantined.

    Notice that the tool did not identify the prodrev.zip file because antivirus software cannot open encrypted files for scanning.

FIGURE 6.8

AVG's Virus Vault

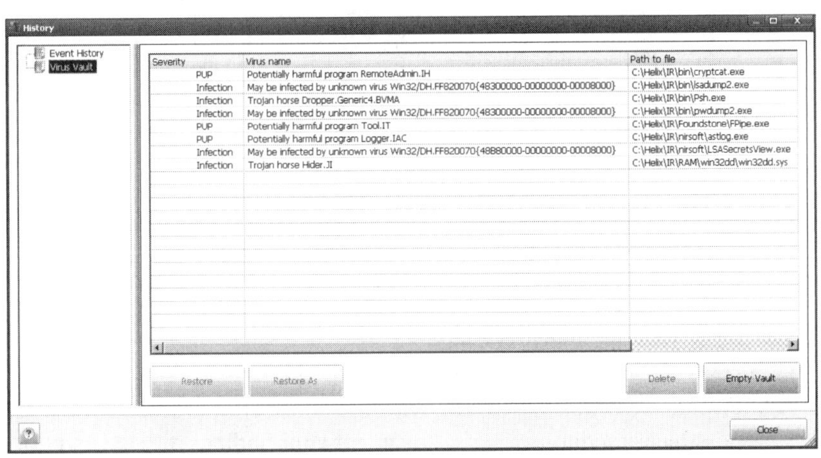

27. **Make a screen capture** of the Virus Vault and **paste** it into your text document.

> **Note:**
> To capture the screen, **press** the **Ctrl** and **PrtSc** keys together, and then **use Ctrl + V** to paste the image into a Word or other word processor document.

28. **Click** the **Empty Vault button** to delete any virus, malware, and malicious software detected by the application.
29. **Click Yes** to confirm the process.
30. **Click Close** to close the Virus Vault.

> **Note:**
> The next steps will detect a hidden virus embedded in an encrypted file. You will use the IZarc Archiver tool to open the file and then use the various tools offered by AVG Business Edition 2012 to inspect the malware or malicious software before removing it.

31. **Maximize** the **ISSA_TOOLS folder**.
32. **Right-click** the **prodrev.zip file**.
33. **Click IZarc** and **Extract Here** from the context menu.

FIGURE 6.9
Extracting the encrypted file

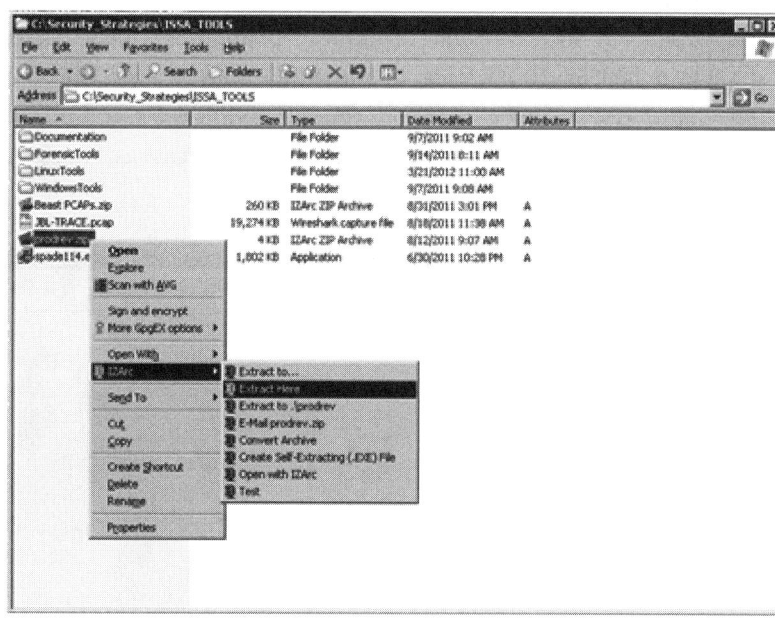

34. When prompted, **type password123** (the document's password) in the password dialog box.
The newly extracted file, productreview.pdf, will appear in the ISSA_TOOLS folder.

35. **Double-click** the **productreview.pdf file** and **type password123** (the document's password) in the password dialog box to open the file.
    AVG, still running in the background, will detect the virus within the file and display an alert message.

FIGURE 6.10

AVG's Threat Detected alert

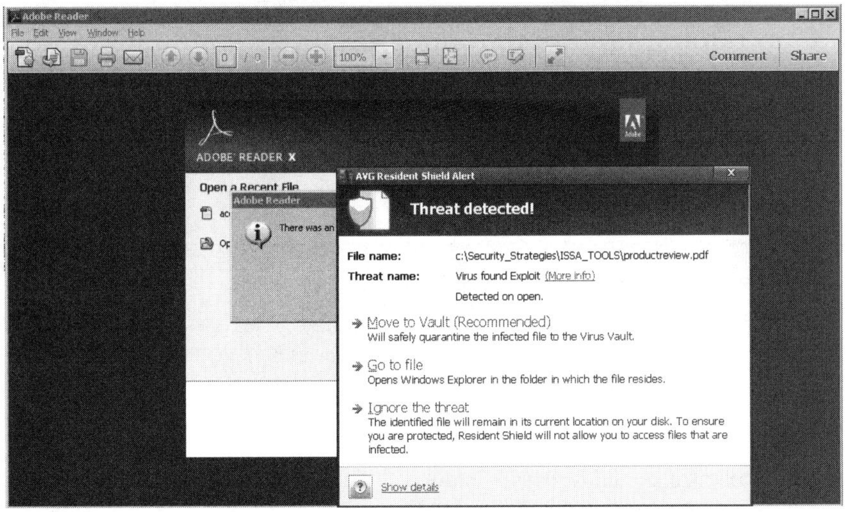

36. **Make a screen capture** of the alert message and **paste** it into your text document.
37. **Click** the **Move to Vault (Recommended)** option to quarantine the file within AVG's vault.
38. **Click Close** to close the alert message.
39. **Click OK** to close the Adobe error message and **close Adobe Reader.**
40. **Close** the **ISSA_TOOLS folder** to bring the AVG software to the forefront.
41. In the AVG toolbar, **click History** and **select Virus Vault.**
42. If necessary, **expand** the **Path to file column width** as necessary to **verify** that the **productreview.pdf file** is displayed in the vault.

FIGURE 6.11

The AVG Virus Vault

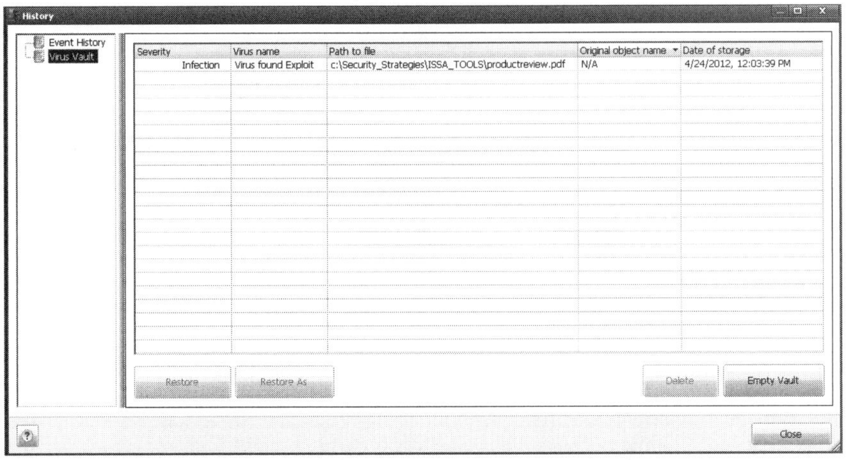

43. **Make a screen capture** of the Virus Vault and **paste** it into your text document.
44. **Click** the **Empty Vault button** to delete any virus, malware, and malicious software detected by the application.
45. **Click Yes** to confirm the process.
46. **Click Close** to close the Virus Vault.
47. **Close** the **AVG window.**
48. Use the **File Transfer button** to download the **text file** to your local computer and submit it as part of your deliverables.

Evaluation Criteria and Rubrics

The following are the evaluation criteria and rubrics for Lab #6 that students must perform:

1. Was the student able to identify malware and other malicious software on a Windows desktop using AVG antivirus and anti-malware tools? – [**20%**]
2. Was the student able to quarantine malware and other malicious software using antivirus and anti-malware for further investigation and removal? – [**20%**]
3. Was the student able to detect a hidden virus embedded in a PDF document with immediate quarantining by an AVG antivirus and anti-malware software tool? – [**20%**]
4. Was the student able to use AVG antivirus and anti-malware software tools to quarantine malware and malicious software in a Virus Vault for inspection and removal? – [**20%**]
5. Was the student able to draft a written report identifying what malware and malicious software was found and what remediation steps are needed to mitigate? – [**20%**]

LAB #6 – ASSESSMENT WORKSHEET

Identify and Mitigate Malware and Malicious Software on a Windows Server

Course Name and Number: ______________________________

Student Name: ______________________________

Instructor Name: ______________________________

Lab Due Date: ______________________________

Overview

In this lab, you used AVG Business Edition 2012, an antivirus and anti-malware software tool, to identify the viruses, Trojans, or malware and malicious software found on a compromised system. Once the malware and malicious software was eliminated, you crafted a summary of findings report describing the problems and your recommendations for remediation.

Lab Assessment Questions & Answers

1. Why is it recommended to do an antivirus signature file update before performing an antivirus scan on your computer?

____

____

____

____

____

2. What are typical indicators that your computer system is compromised?

____

____

____

____

____

____

3. Where does AVG Business Edition 2012 place viruses, Trojans, worms, and other malicious software when it finds them?

4. What other viruses, Trojans, worms, or malicious software were identified and quarantined by AVG within the Virus Vault upon completion of the Whole Computer Scan?

5. What elements are needed in a workstation domain policy regarding use of antivirus and malicious software prevention tools?

Conduct a Network Traffic Analysis and Baseline Definition

LAB 7

Introduction

In this lab, you will create and capture traffic from the machines in this lab using tcpdump, a command line packet analyzer, and the Wireshark protocol capture and analyzer tool. You also will open Telnet and SSH sessions and use FileZilla and the Tftpd32 application to transfer files between the virtual machines. You will use NetWitness Investigator, a free tool that provides security practitioners with a means of analyzing packets to view the data captured using Wireshark.

Learning Objectives

Upon completing this lab, you will be able to:

- Use Wireshark and NetWitness Investigator as a packet capture and protocol analysis tool
- Capture live IP, ICMP, TCP, and UDP traffic using Telnet, FTP, TFTP, and SSH sessions
- Examine captured packet traces to view cleartext and ciphertext
- Analyze the packet capture data in both Wireshark and NetWitness Investigator and be able to identify the difference between UDP and TCP sessions
- Identify common network-related protocols used for client-server communications, network management, and network security

TOOLS AND SOFTWARE

NAME	MORE INFORMATION
FileZilla Server and FileZilla Client	http://filezilla-project.org/
NetWitness Investigator	http://www.emc.com/security/rsa-netwitness.htm
PuTTY	http://www.chiark.greenend.org.uk/~sgtatham/putty/
TCPdump	http://tcpdump.org
Tftpd32	http://tftpd32.jounin.net/
Wireshark	http://www.wireshark.org/

Deliverables

Upon completion of this lab, you are required to provide the following deliverables to your instructor:

1. A text document containing each of the following items:
   a. A screen capture of the tcpdump capture of the TargetUbuntu01 server;
   b. An explanation of the difference between SSH and Telnet;
   c. An explanation of the difference between FTP and TFTP;
   d. An explanation of the difference between secure and unsecure connections and a list of the logons and passwords captured in this lab;
2. Lab #7.pcap (the Wireshark protocol traffic file);
3. Lab Assessment Questions & Answers for Lab #7.

Hands-On Steps

1. This lab begins at the student landing vWorkstation virtual machine desktop of the VSCL, as shown here.

FIGURE 7.1

"Student Landing" VSCL workstation

Note:

The next steps will use the tcpdump utility to capture network traffic on the TargetUbuntu01 virtual Linux server. You will generate that traffic using the Damn Vulnerable Web Application (DVWA) tool.

2. **Double-click** the **ISSA_VM Server Farm_RDP icon** on the desktop. This folder contains links to the virtual servers in this lab environment.
3. **Double-click** the **TargetUbuntu01 icon** to a remote desktop connection to the Linux server.

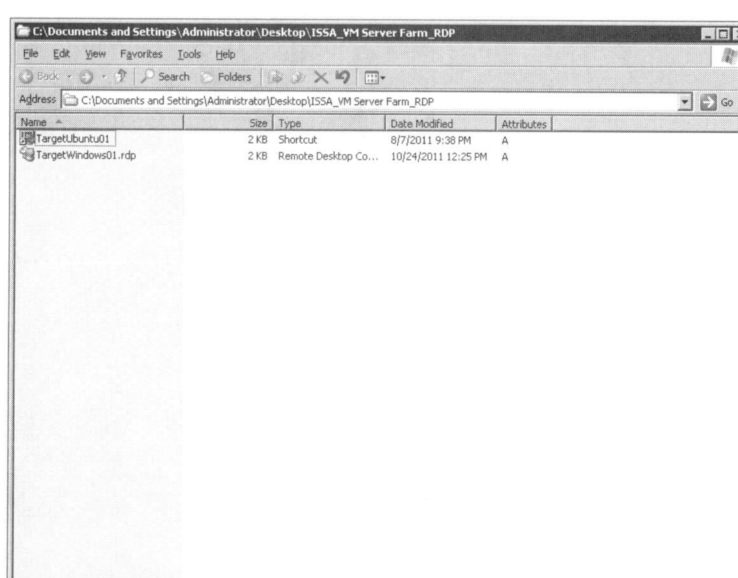

FIGURE 7.2

Open a remote desktop connection to TargetUbuntu01

7 Conduct a Network Traffic Analysis and Baseline Definition

4. **Log in** to the **TargetUbuntu01 VM** server with the following credentials:
   - User name: **student**
   - Password: **ISS316Security**

FIGURE 7.3

Connecting to TargetUbuntu01 server

5. From the Linux toolbar, **click Applications**, **click Accessories**, and **select Terminal** to open the Linux command prompt.
6. At the command prompt, **type sudo -i** to use the superuser account, instead of the student account, to access the root directory.
7. When prompted for a password, **type ISS316Security**.

   The command prompt will change from *student@targetubuntu*:~$ to *root@targetubuntu*:~# indicating the change was successful.
8. At the command prompt, **type man tcpdump** to open the onscreen manual for the tcpdump utility.

   This screen displays all of the command line options for the tool and descriptions for each. Use the arrow keys to scroll through the manual to learn more about this tool.

   Press CTRL and **type Z** to return to the command line prompt.

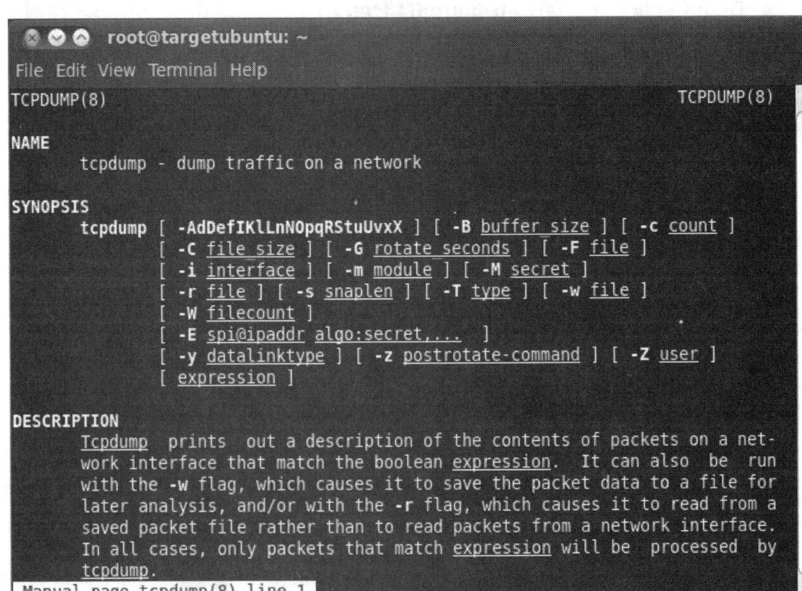

FIGURE 7.4

The default screen for tcpdump

9. At the command prompt, **type cd /etc/network** to change the directory.
10. At the command prompt, **type ls** to list the files in that directory.
11. At the command prompt, **type cat interfaces** to display the available Ethernet interfaces.

    The system returns the list of Ethernet interfaces available. Verify that eth0 (the physical Internet interface) is available by looking for the following statement in the results:

    - **iface etho0 inet static**
12. Document the IP address that appears in this series of statements: (*address* = ____________________). You will need this for a later step.
13. At the command prompt, **type cd** to return to the root directory.
14. At the command prompt, **type tcpdump –i eth0 –n –w lab7tcpdump** to start the data capture. This command also instructs the utility to save the results of the data capture to a file (lab7tcpdump) instead of printing the results.

    The tcpdump utility is now configured to capture data on the eth0 interface.

FIGURE 7.5

Capturing data using the tcpdump utility

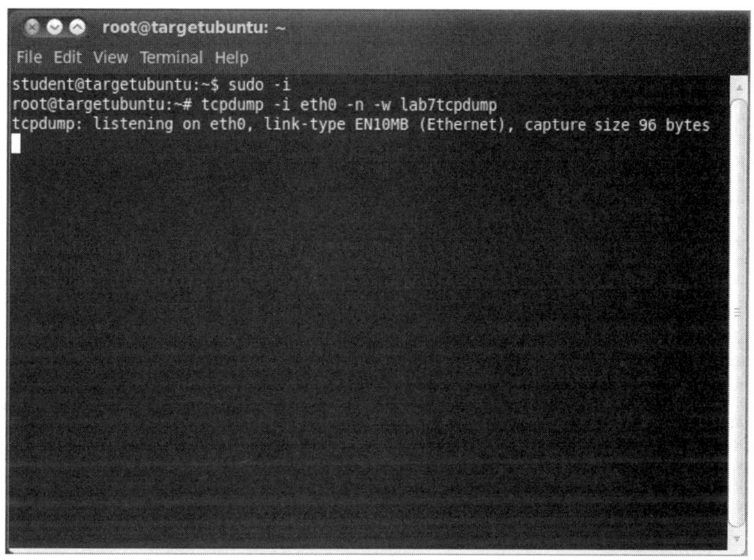

15. **Minimize** the **TargetUbuntu01 window** to return to the vWorkstation desktop.
16. **Double-click** the **Mozilla Firefox icon** on the desktop to open the Firefox browser.

    You can access the DVWA tool using any Internet browser, but the steps in this lab will use the Firefox browser.

17. In the browser's address box, **type http://*address*/dvwa**, using the IP address you documented in step 12, and **press Enter**.

FIGURE 7.6

DVWA login screen

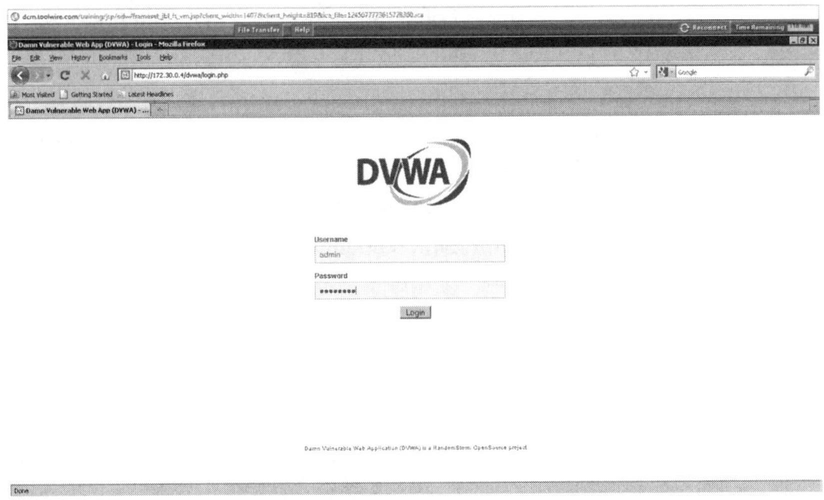

18. Log in to the application with the following credentials and **click Login** to continue:
    - Username: **admin**
    - Password: **password**
19. On the DVWA Welcome screen, **click** the **DVWA Security button**.
20. **Select low** from the Script Security drop-down menu. **Click Submit** to change the security level.

FIGURE 7.7

Changing the script security level in DVWA

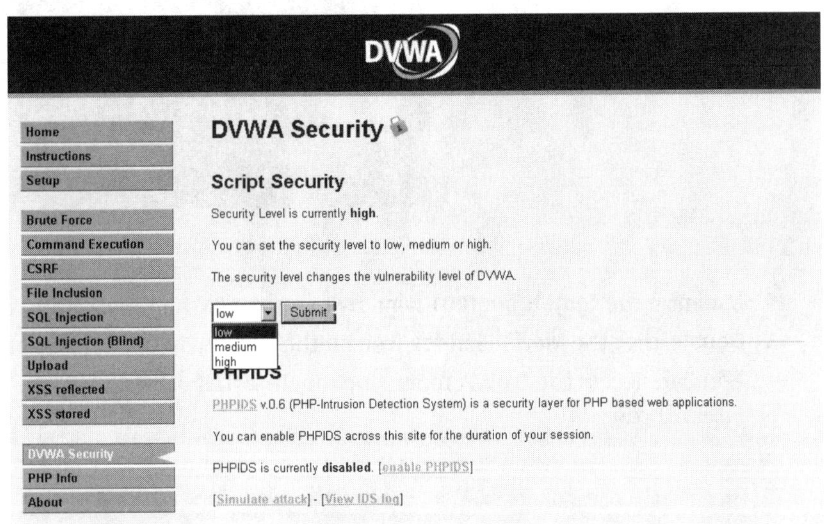

21. **Generate data** for the tcpdump by **repeating steps 7 through 30 from Lab #5**, *Perform a Website and Database Attack by Exploiting Identified Vulnerabilities*, earlier in this lab. Note that you will not have to repeat the screen captures for this lab.
22. **Maximize** the **TargetUbuntu01 window** to return to that server.
23. In the terminal window, **press CTRL** and **type Z** to stop the data capture and return to the command line prompt.

24. At the terminal command prompt, **type tcpdump –n -r lab7tcpdump** to display the contents of the lab7tcpdump file.

FIGURE 7.8

Displaying the results of the data capture

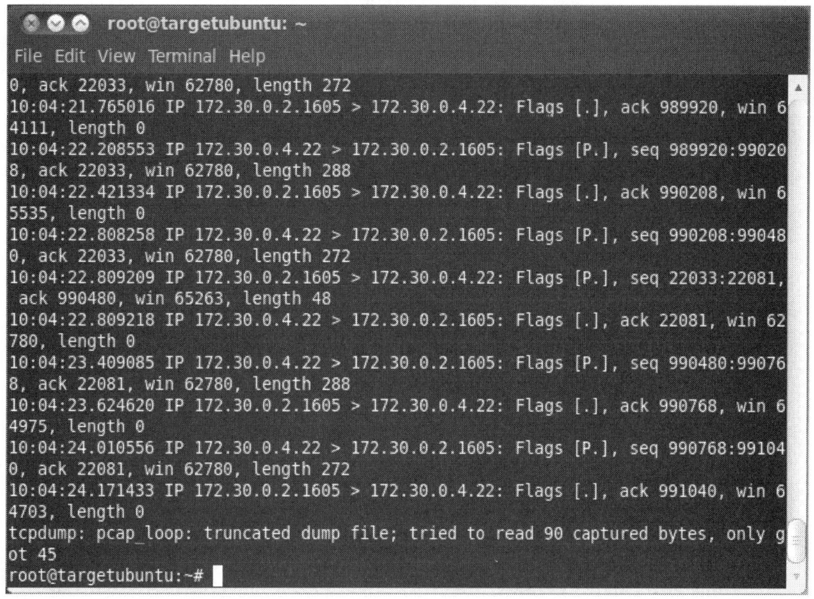

25. **Make a screen capture** of this screen and **paste** it into a new text document. **Submit** it to your instructor as a deliverable.

> **Note:**
> To capture the screen, **press** the **Ctrl** and **PrtSc** keys together, and then **use Ctrl + V** to paste the image into a Word or other word processor document.

26. **Close** the **terminal window**.
27. **Click** the **Close Terminal button** to close the terminal window.
28. **Minimize** the **TargetUbuntu01 window**.

> **Note:**
> The next steps will use the Wireshark application to capture and analyze TCP/IP traffic. You will then use the PuTTY application to establish a Telnet or SSH connection to the IP addresses for several of the machines available in this lab. Each of these connections will gather more data for Wireshark to capture.

29. **Double-click** the **Wireshark icon** on the desktop to start that application.

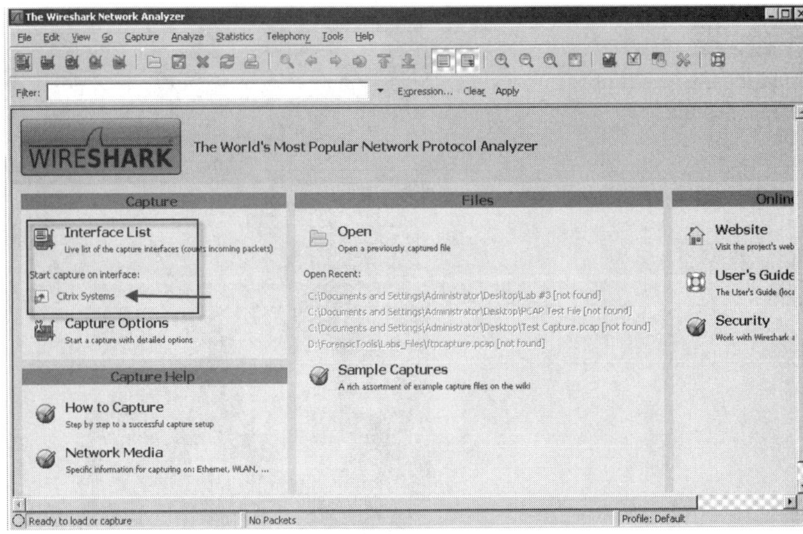

FIGURE 7.9

The Wireshark window

30. **Click** the **Citrix Systems link** in the Interface List section of the application window. Wireshark automatically begins capturing data from any open connections.

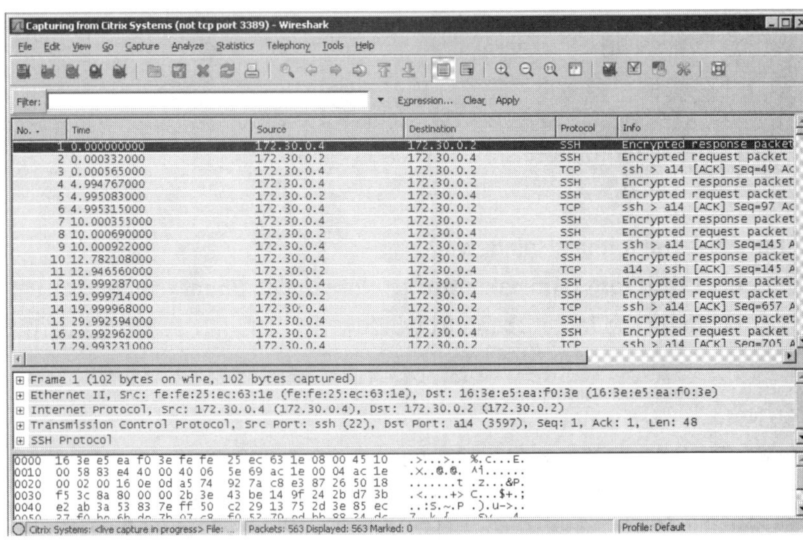

FIGURE 7.10

Data from the Wireshark capture

31. **Minimize** the **Wireshark application**.
32. **Double-click** the **PuTTY icon** on the desktop to start the PuTTY application.

    You will open connections to several of the machines in the virtual lab environment. Any activities you perform during this session will generate more data for the data packet captured by Wireshark.
33. In the PuTTY application window, **type** the IP address for LAN Switch 1, **172.16.8.5**. **Select** the **Telnet radio button** and **type 23** in the Port box. **Click** the **Open button** to start the connection.

FIGURE 7.11

PuTTY application window

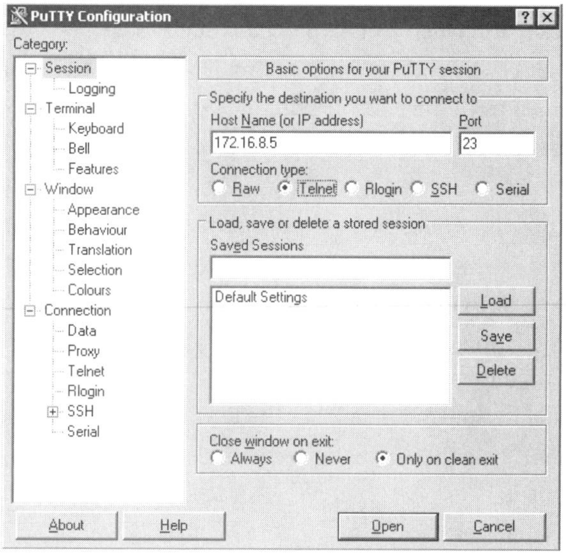

34. PuTTY will launch a terminal console window. At the login prompt, **type** the following credentials:
    - User name: **cisco**
    - Password: **cisco**

FIGURE 7.12

PuTTY terminal console window

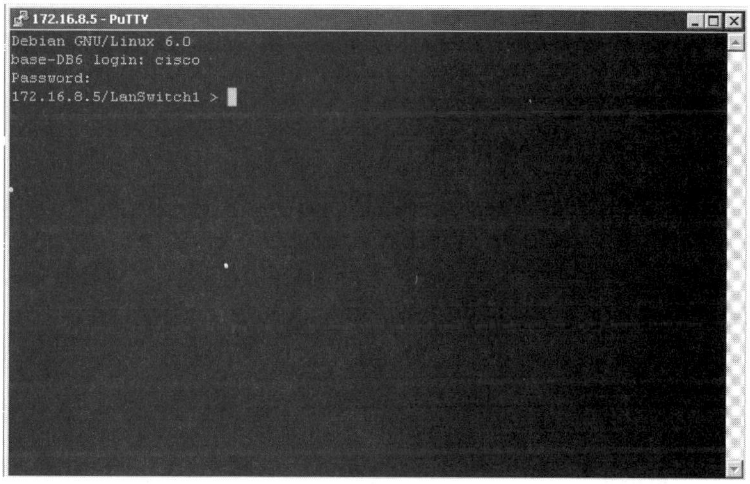

35. In the terminal console window, **type show interface** to display the list of available interfaces.
36. In the terminal console window, **type show vlan** to display the VLANs on this machine.
37. In the terminal console window, **type quit** to close the terminal console.
38. **Repeat steps 32–37** for each of the following IP addresses:
    - LAN Switch 2: **172.16.20.5**
    - Tampa 2811 router: **172.17.8.1**
39. **Double-click** the **PuTTY icon** on the desktop to start the PuTTY application.
40. In the PuTTY application window, **type** the IP address for the Norfolk 2811 router, **172.16.8.1. Select** the **SSH radio button** and **type 22** in the Port box. **Click** the **Open button** to start the connection.

    You will receive a PuTTY Security Alert asking if you trust the host. **Click** the **Yes** button to continue.
41. PuTTY will launch a terminal console window. At the login prompt, **type** the following credentials:
    - User name: **cisco**
    - Password: **cisco**
42. In the terminal console window, **type show interface** to display the list of available interfaces.
43. In the terminal console window, **type show vlan** to display the VLANs on this machine.
44. In the terminal console window, **type quit** to close the terminal console.
45. In the PuTTY application window, **type *address*** using the IP address for the TargetUbuntu01 server that you documented in step 12.
46. **Select** the **SSH radio button** and **type 22** in the Port box. **Click** the **Open button** to start the connection.
47. At the login prompt, **type** the following credentials:
    - User name: **student**
    - Password: **ISS316Security**
48. In the terminal console window, **type exit** to close the terminal console.
49. In your text document, **explain** the **difference between SSH and Telnet**.

> **Note:**
> The next steps will open a connection to the TargetWindows01 server and gather additional packet data by using the Tftpd32 application and FileZilla to send several small files between clients and servers on the various machines.

50. In the ISSA_VM Server Farm_RDP window, **double-click** the **TargetWindows01.rdp file** to open a connection to the Windows server.
51. **Log on** to the **TargetWindows01 VM** server with the following credentials:
    - User name: **Administrator**
    - Password: **ISS316Security**

52. **Click OK** in the Connect to Server dialog box to start the FileZilla Server application.

    This dialog box loads automatically when the Windows server starts, with the address and password already filled in.

FIGURE 7.13

Connect to Server dialog box

53. **Verify** that the FileZilla application is running.

FIGURE 7.14

The FileZilla application window

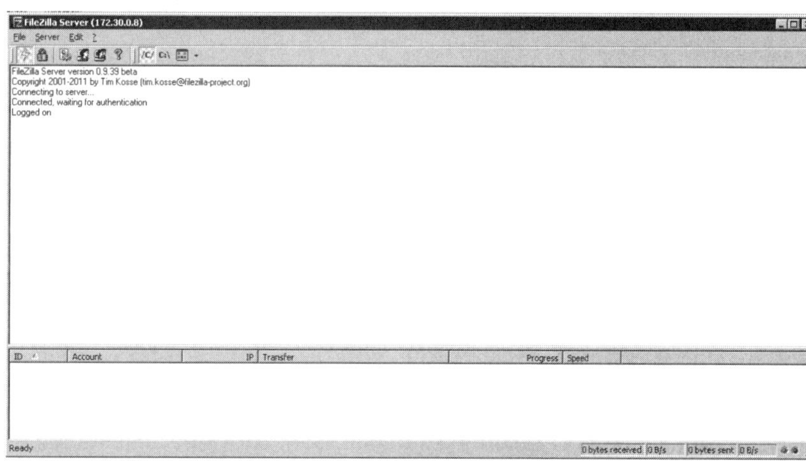

If the FileZilla application is not running, you can open it by **double-clicking** on the **FileZilla Server Interface icon** on the TargetWindows01 desktop.

54. **Minimize** the **TargetWindows01 desktop**.
55. **Double-click** the **FileZilla icon** on the vWorkstation desktop.
56. **Type** the following login credentials in the address boxes at the top of the application window that opens to connect to the FileZilla Server on the TargetWindows01 server.

    Host: **172.30.0.8**

    User name: **student**

    Password: **ISS316Security**

    Port: **21**
57. **Click** the **Quickconnect button** to connect to the FileZilla Server.

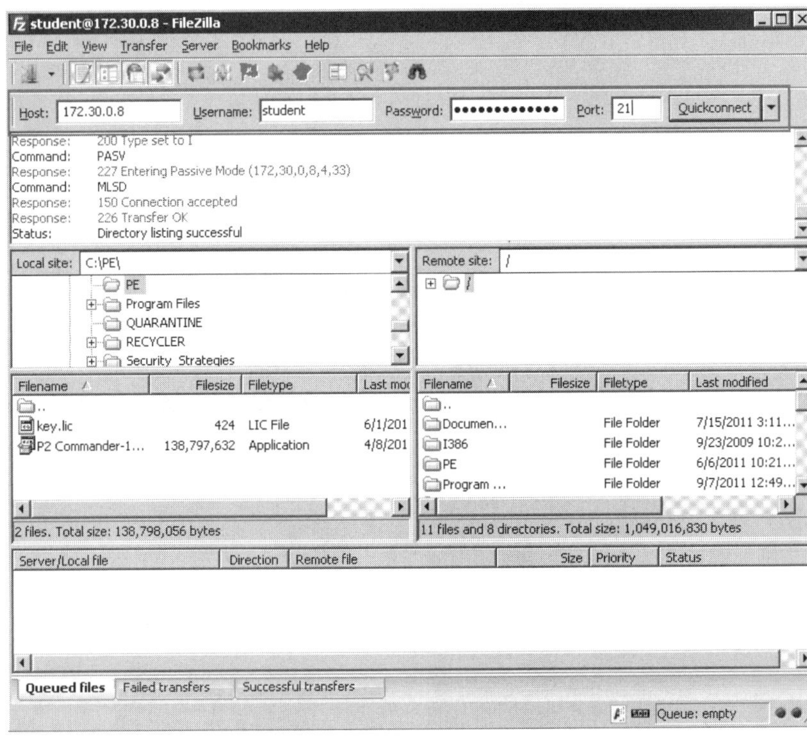

FIGURE 7.15 Connecting to TargetWindows01 using FileZilla

58. **Navigate** to the **C:\Security_Strategies\ISSA_TOOLS\Documentation folder** in the Local site (vWorkstation) directory.
59. **Select** the **AnyConnect_adminguide.pdf file**.

60. **Drag** the **AnyConnect_adminguide.pdf file** and **drop** it into the **root directory folder** in the Remote site (TargetWindows01) pane.

    The status responses in the area below the connection information indicate whether or not the file transfer was successful.

FIGURE 7.16

Successful FTP from vWorkstation to TargetWindows01

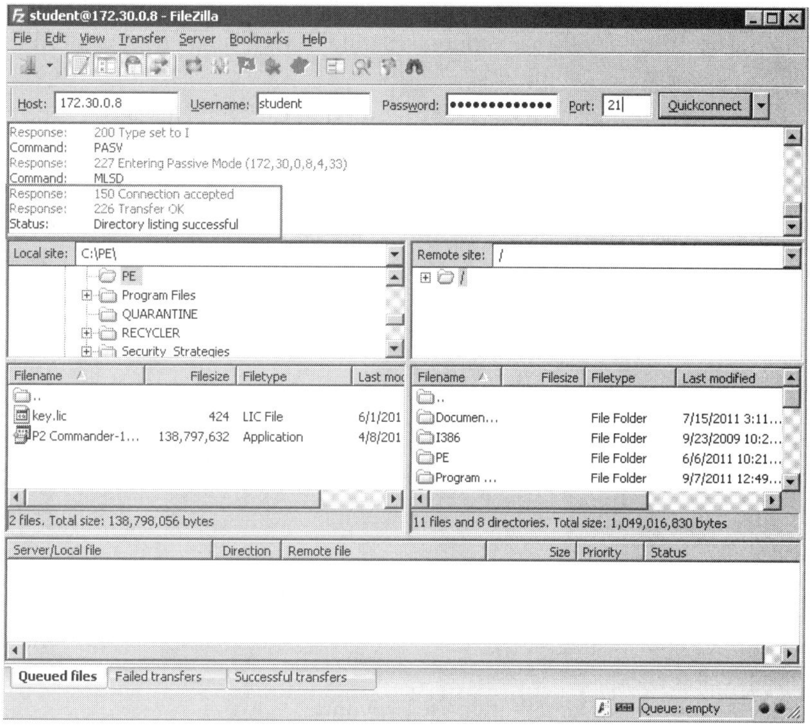

61. **Maximize** the **TargetWindows01 desktop** and verify that the file was transferred.

FIGURE 7.17

Successful FTP transfer of the AnyConnect_adminguide.pdf file

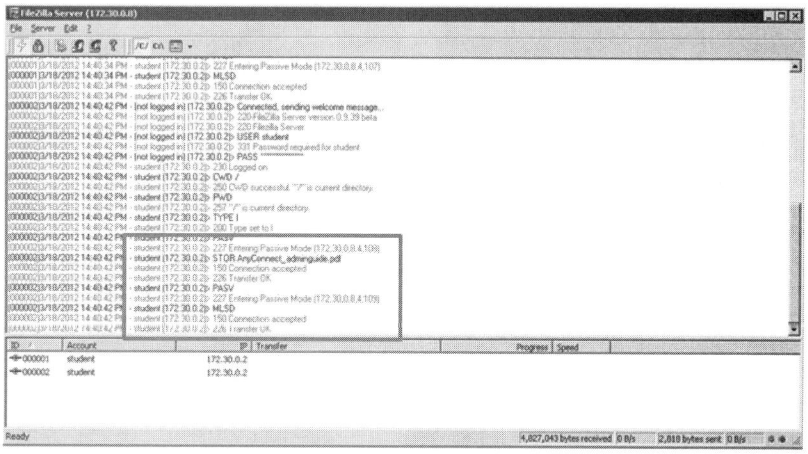

62. **Close** the **FileZilla Server window**.
63. **Double-click** the **Tftpd32_SE Admin icon** on the TargetWindows01 desktop.
64. When the application window launches, **click** the **Tftp Client tab**.
65. **Minimize** the **TargetWindows01 window** to return to the vWorkstation desktop.
66. **Close** the **FileZilla window**.
67. **Double-click** the **Tftpd32_SE Admin icon** to launch the application.

    The Tftpd32_SE application uses the TFTP (Trivial File Transfer Protocol) to send (put) or receive (get) files between computers.
68. When the application window launches, **click** the **Tftp Server tab**.

FIGURE 7.18

The Tftpd32 application

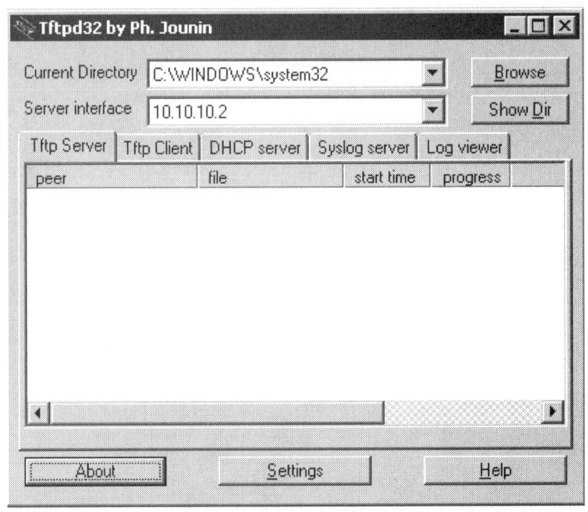

69. **Maximize** the **TargetWindows01 window**.
70. On the Tftp Client tab, **type or select** the following information and click the **Put button** to set up the TargetWindows01 server as the Tftp client (or receiving computer):
    - Host: **172.30.0.2** (vWorkstation)
    - Port: **69**
    - Local File: **C:\AnyConnect_adminguide.pdf**
    - Block Size: **Default**

    This is the same file that you transferred using FileZilla earlier in this lab. The status responses in the area below the connection information indicate whether or not the file transfer was successful.
71. **Close** the **Tftpd32 application**.
72. **Minimize** the **TargetWindows01 window** to return to the vWorkstation desktop.
73. **Close** the **Tftpd32 application** on the vWorkstation desktop.
74. In your text document, **explain** the **difference between FTP and TFTP**.

> **Note:**
> The next steps will stop the data capture that Wireshark has been collecting, and save a .pcap file for analysis later in this lab. You will need this file as a deliverable for this lab.

75. **Maximize** the **Wireshark application**, if necessary.
76. **Click** the **Stop the running live capture icon** on the Wireshark toolbar to stop the packet capture process.
77. **Click** the **Save icon** to save the packet capture. When the "Wireshark: Save file as" dialog box opens, **name** the file **Lab #7** and **select Wireshark/tcpdump...libpcap [*.pcap, *.cap]** from the "Save as type" menu. **Save** the file to the Security_Strategies folder (**My Computer > Local Disk (C:) > Security_Strategies**).
78. Use the **File Transfer button** to download the **Lab #7.pcap file** to your local computer and submit it as part of your deliverables.
79. **Close** the **Wireshark application**.

> **Note:**
> The next steps will use NetWitness Investigator to view the Wireshark packet capture you just saved. NetWitness Investigator allows you to look at and analyze packet capture data in context, so that you are able to act on any threats or problems quickly and easily. These steps show you how to build a NetWitness Investigator local collection, which you can use to analyze and submit your packet capture data to your instructor as part of the lab deliverables.

80. **Double-click** the **NetWitness Investigator icon** on the vWorkstation desktop to start the application.
81. When the application window launches, **click Collection** in the toolbar and **select New Local Collection**.
82. In the New Local Collection dialog box, **name** the collection **Lab #7** and save it to the default location by **clicking OK**.

    A new collection named Lab #7 will appear at the bottom of the collection list in the left pane of the application window.

FIGURE 7.19
New Local Collection dialog box

83. **Double-click** on the new **Lab #7** collection to change the status to **Ready**.

84. **Right-click** on the new **Lab #7** collection and **select Import Packets** from the context menu.

FIGURE 7.20

Importing a PCAP file into NetWitness Investigator

85. In the Open dialog box, **navigate** to the Security_Strategies folder (**My Computer > Local Disk (C:) > Security_Strategies**) and **select** the **Lab #7.pcap file**. **Click Open** to import the file

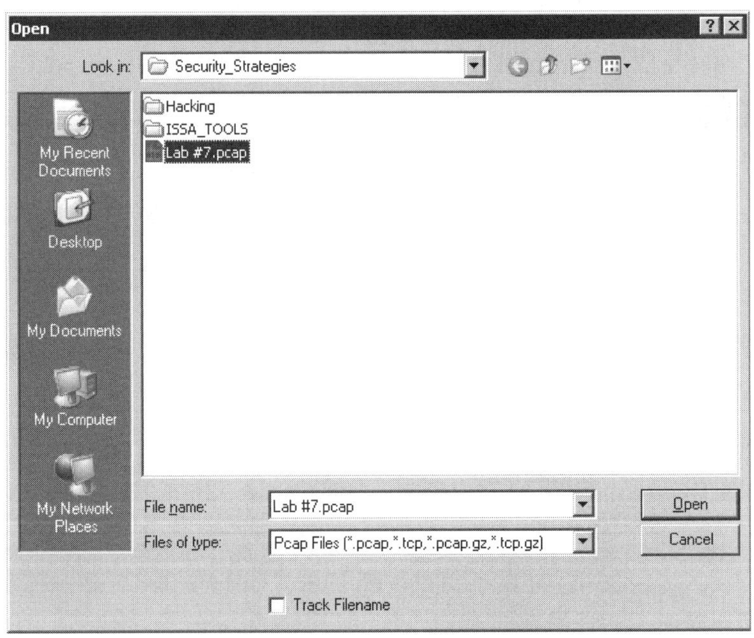

FIGURE 7.21

Opening the Lab #7. pcap file

86. **Double-click** the new **Lab #7** collection to review the information captured by Wireshark.

FIGURE 7.22

Summary information

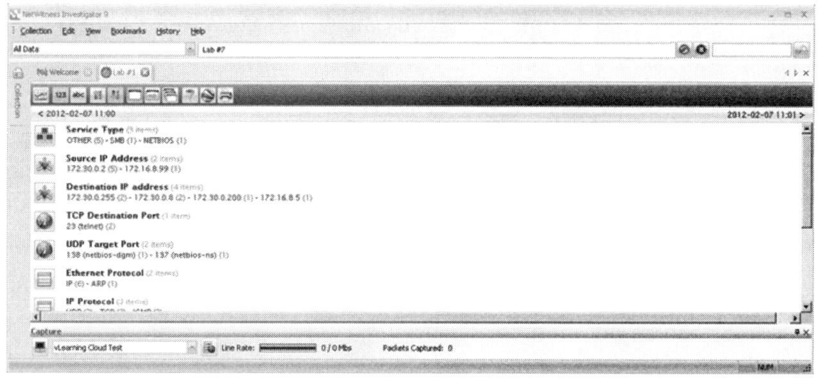

87. **Close** the **NetWitness Investigator window**.
88. In your text document, **include an explanation** of the difference between secure and unsecure connections and a list of the logons and passwords captured in this lab.
89. Use the **File Transfer button** to download your **text document** to your local computer and submit it as part of your deliverables.

Evaluation Criteria and Rubrics

The following are the evaluation criteria and rubrics for Lab #7 that the students must perform:

1. Was the student able to use Wireshark and NetWitness Investigator as a packet capture and protocol analysis tool? – **[20%]**
2. Was the student able to capture live IP, ICMP, TCP, and UDP traffic using Telnet, FTP, TFTP, and SSH sessions? – **[20%]**
3. Was the student able to examine captured packet traces to view cleartext and ciphertext? – **[20%]**
4. Was the student able to analyze the packet capture data in both Wireshark and NetWitness Investigator and identify the difference between UDP and TCP sessions? – **[20%]**
5. Was the student able to identify common network-related protocols used for client-server communications, network management, and network security? – **[20%]**

LAB #7 – ASSESSMENT WORKSHEET

Conduct a Network Traffic Analysis and Baseline Definition

Course Name and Number: ______________________________

Student Name: ______________________________

Instructor Name: ______________________________

Lab Due Date: ______________________________

Overview

In this lab, you created and captured traffic from the machines in this lab using tcpdump, a command line packet analyzer, and the Wireshark protocol capture and analyzer tool. You opened Telnet and SSH sessions and used FileZilla and the Tftpd32 application to transfer files between the virtual machines. You used NetWitness Investigator, a free tool that provides security practitioners with a means of analyzing packets to view the data captured using Wireshark.

Lab Assessment Questions & Answers

1. Which tool is better at performing protocol captures and which tool is better at performing protocol analysis?

____

____

____

____

2. What is the significance of the TCP three-way handshake for applications that utilize TCP as a transport protocol? Which application in your protocol capture uses TCP as a transport protocol?

3. How many different source IP host addresses did you capture in your protocol capture?

4. How many different protocols (layer 3, layer 4, etc.) did your protocol capture session have? What function in Wireshark provides you with a breakdown of the different protocol types on the LAN segment?

5. Can Wireshark provide you with network traffic packet size counts? How and where? Are you able to distinguish how many of each packet size was transmitted on your LAN segment? Why is this important to know?

6. Why is it important to use protocol capture tools and protocol analyzers as an information systems security professional?

7. What are some challenges to protocol analysis and network traffic analysis?

8. Why would an information systems security practitioner want to see network traffic on both internal and external LAN segments at the DMZ within the LAN-to-WAN domain (i.e., both on the inside and outside LAN segments)?

Audit and Implement a Secure WLAN Solution

LAB 8

Introduction

In this lab, you will explore how the Aircrack-ng suite of tools, a set of WLAN hacking applications, can be used to compromise WLAN security implementations. You will download a video that demonstrates the use of these tools in identifying cleartext and cracking passwords on a WLAN. This video explains different initialization vectors (IVs) and points of entry into an unprotected or weakly protected WLAN and how to recover an unencrypted WEP key. You also will use the information from this lab to craft a WLAN security implementation plan that will mitigate any weaknesses and security threats commonly found in a WLAN implementation.

Learning Objectives

Upon completing this lab, you will be able to:

- Review WLAN protocol scans, and identify wireless access points that may be open or using a weak encryption standard
- Perform a security assessment on a WLAN implementation using WEP/WPA/WPA2 encryption implementations on a wireless access point
- Review BackTrack4 and the Aircrack-ng suite of tools to decrypt previously captured scans and captures of WLAN traffic and WLAN encryption
- Mitigate weaknesses and security threats commonly found in WLAN implementations with proper security countermeasures
- Craft a WLAN security implementation plan to address confidentiality, integrity, and availability of WLAN services

TOOLS AND SOFTWARE

NAME	MORE INFORMATION
Aircrack-ng	http://www.aircrack-ng.org/

Deliverables

Upon completion of this lab, you are required to provide the following deliverables to your instructor:

1. A text document that includes each of the following items:
   a. A summary of the functions of each of the hacking tools explored in this lab;
   b. An explanation of initialization vectors (IV) and their importance;
   c. The WEP key identified by the Aircrack–ng tool in the demonstration video;
   d. A summary of the steps used in the video for cracking the WEP key;
2. A WLAN security implementation plan that contains each of the following items:
   a. A summary of findings;
   b. A list of critical risks, threats, and vulnerabilities;
   c. A security assessment;
   d. A list of security recommendations;
3. Lab Assessment Questions & Answers for Lab #8.

Hands-On Steps

1. This lab begins at the student landing vWorkstation virtual machine desktop of the VSCL, as shown here.

FIGURE 8.1

"Student Landing" VSCL workstation

> **Note:**
> The next steps establish a remote connection to the BackTrack4 virtual machine and then explore the online manual for each of the hacking application tools included in the Aircrack –ng suite of tools. You will familiarize yourself with the available switches for each.

2. **Double-click** the **ISSA_VM Server Farm_RDP icon** on the desktop. This folder contains links to the virtual servers in this lab environment.
3. **Double-click** the **BackTrack4 icon** to a remote desktop connection to that machine.

FIGURE 8.2

Open a remote desktop connection to BackTrack4

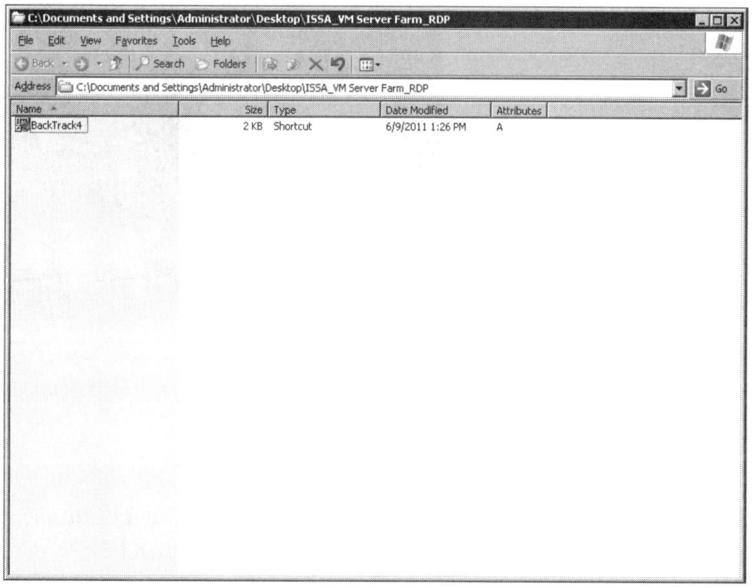

4. **Log in** to the **BackTrack4 VM** server with the following credentials:
   - User name: **root**
   - Password: **toor**

FIGURE 8.3

BackTrack4 login screen

5. **Click** the **Konsole Terminal Program icon** in the toolbar at the bottom of the window.
6. At the command prompt, **type man airmon-ng** to review the online manual for this tool.

FIGURE 8.4

The online manual for airmon-ng

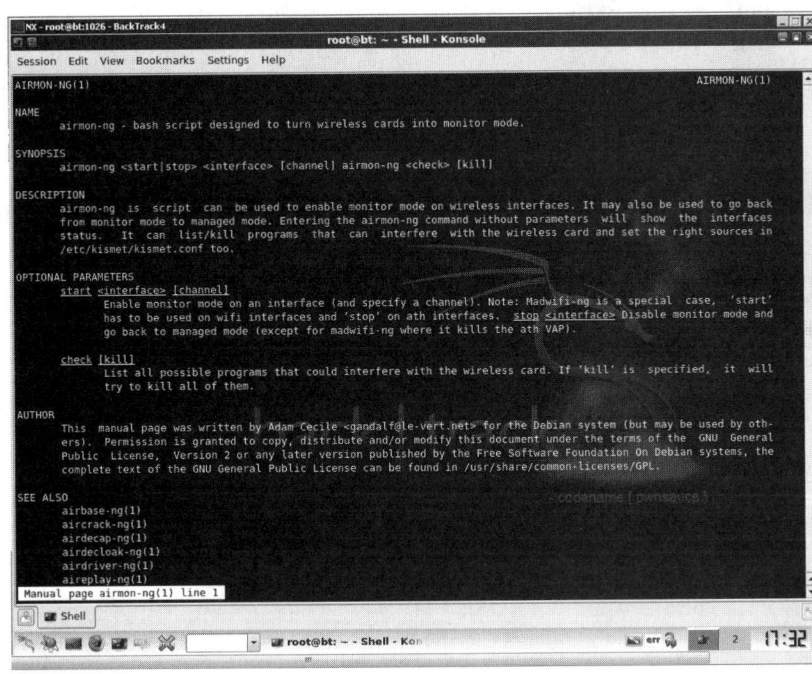

7. **Use** the **scrollbar** at the right of the screen to explore the functions and switches for this tool. You will need this information as part of your deliverables for this lab.
8. At the command prompt, **type q** to return to the terminal prompt.

9. At the command prompt, **type airodump-ng - -help** to review the online manual for this tool.

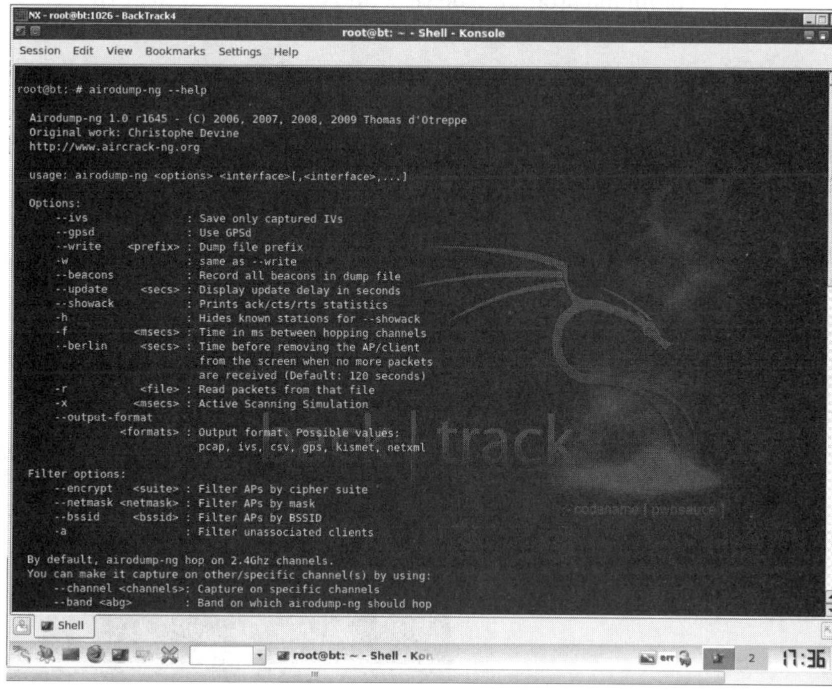

FIGURE 8.5

The help screen for airodump-ng

10. **Use** the **scrollbar** at the right of the screen to explore the functions and switches for this tool. You will need this information as part of your deliverables for this lab.
11. At the command prompt, **type clear** and **press Enter** to clear the screen and return to the terminal prompt.
12. At the command prompt, **type aireplay-ng - -help** to review the online manual for this tool.

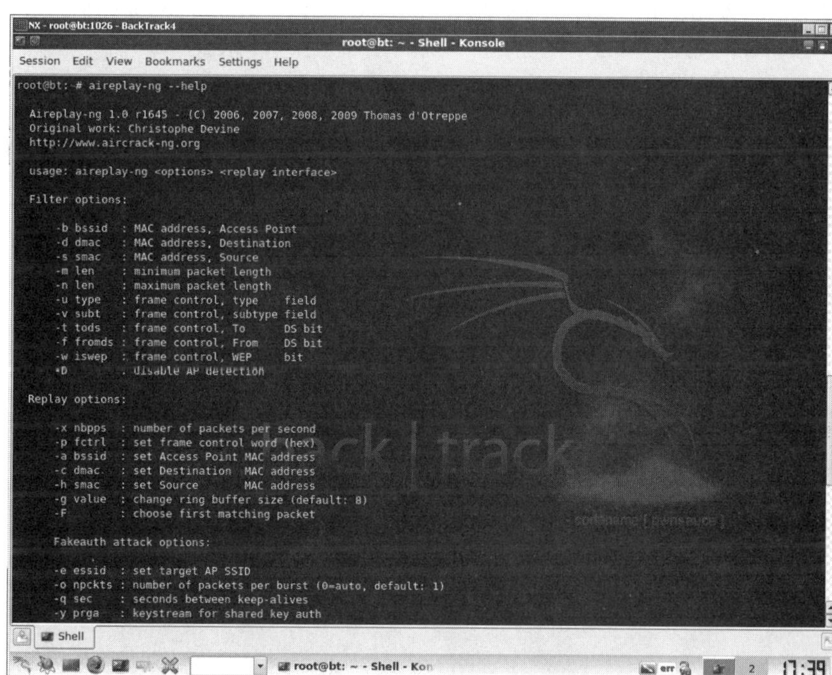

FIGURE 8.6

The help screen for aireplay-ng

13. **Use** the **scrollbar** at the right of the screen to explore the functions and switches for this tool. You will need this information as part of your deliverables for this lab.
14. At the command prompt, **type clear** and **press Enter** to clear the screen and return to the terminal prompt.
15. At the command prompt, **type aircrack-ng - -help** to open the online manual for this tool.

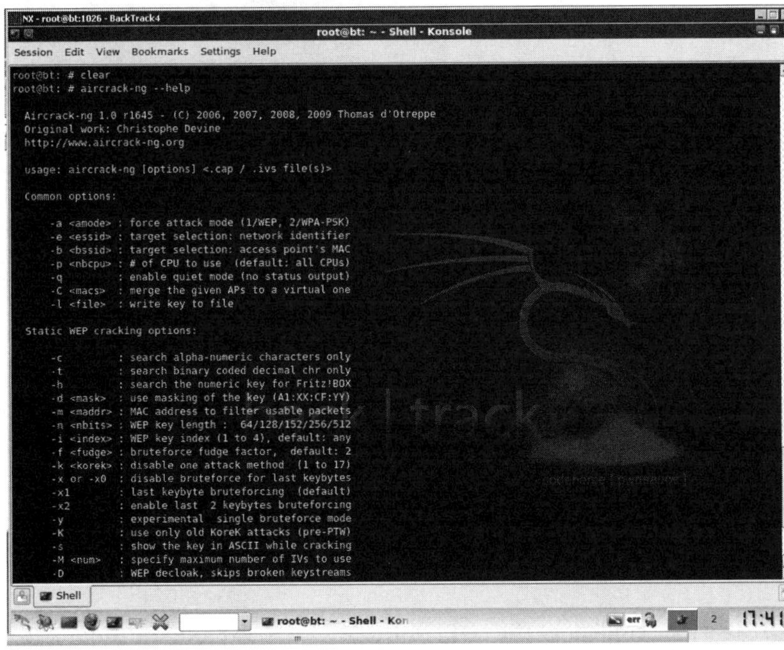

FIGURE 8.7

The help screen for aircrack-ng

16. **Use** the **scrollbar** at the right of the screen to explore the functions and switches for this tool. You will need this information as part of your deliverables for this lab.
17. **Close** the **Konsole window**.
18. **Minimize** the **BackTrack4 window** to return to the vWorkstation desktop.
19. **Click** the **File Transfer button** to download the **Hacking Lab 8 Video.zip file (C:/Security_Strategies/Hacking/Hacking Lab 8 Video.zip)** to your local computer.

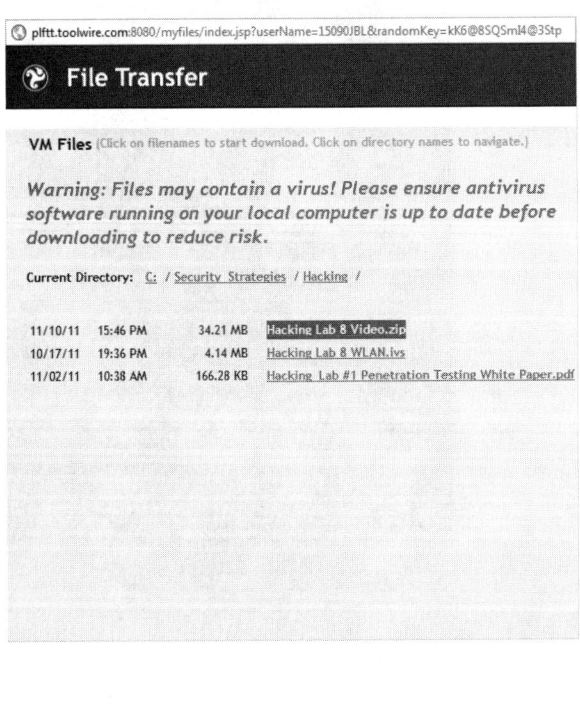

FIGURE 8.8

Transferring the Hacking Lab 8 Video.zip file

20. Use a file extractor to **unzip** the **files** to a new folder on your local computer. Note that for the video and audio in this file to work properly, you must save all four files from this zipped file to the same folder.
21. In a Web browser on your local computer, **open** the **IS4560_Lab8_Alpha.htm file.**
22. **Click** the **play button** in the embedded video window to play a video demonstrating how the hacking tools you explored earlier in this lab can be used to penetrate a vulnerable system.

    You will need the information in this video to complete the deliverables for this lab so you may have to review the video multiple times.

FIGURE 8.9

Viewing the IS4560_Lab8_Alpha.htm file

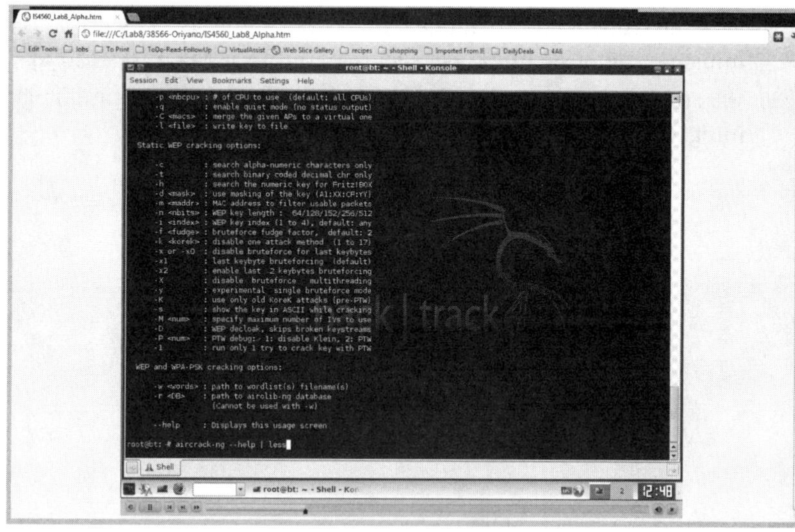

23. **Make a screen capture** of the WEP key identified by the Aircrack–ng tool in the demonstration video and **paste** it into a new text document.

> **Note:**
> To capture the screen, **press** the **Ctrl** and **PrtSc** keys together, and then **use Ctrl + V** to paste the image into a Word or other word processor document.

24. In your text document, **include** an **explanation of initialization vectors (IV) and their importance** to WLAN security.
25. In your text document, **include** a **summary of the steps used in the video for cracking the WEP key** and **submit** the **document** to your instructor as a deliverable for this lab.
26. In a new text document, **create** a **WLAN Security Implementation Plan** to mitigate the identified risks, threats, and vulnerabilities identified by this lab. The document should include each of the following items. **Submit** the document to your instructor as a deliverable for this lab:
    a. A summary of findings
    b. A list of critical risks, threats, and vulnerabilities
    c. A security assessment
    d. Security recommendations

Evaluation Criteria and Rubrics

The following are the evaluation criteria and rubrics for Lab #8 that students must perform:

1. Was the student able to review WLAN protocol scans, and identify wireless access points that may be open or using a weak encryption standard? – [**20%**]
2. Was the student able to perform a security assessment on a WLAN implementation using WEP/WPA/WPA2 encryption implementations on a wireless access point? – [**20%**]
3. Was the student able to use BackTrack4 and the Aircrack-ng suite of tools to decrypt previously captured scans and captures of WLAN traffic and WLAN encryption? – [**20%**]
4. Was the student able to mitigate weaknesses and security threats commonly found in WLAN implementations with proper security countermeasures? – [**20%**]
5. Was the student able to craft a WLAN security implementation plan to address confidentiality, integrity, and availability of WLAN services? – [**20%**]

LAB #8 – ASSESSMENT WORKSHEET

Audit and Implement a Secure WLAN Solution

Course Name and Number: ______________________________

Student Name: ______________________________

Instructor Name: ______________________________

Lab Due Date: ______________________________

Overview

In this lab, you explored how the Aircrack-ng suite of tools, a set of WLAN hacking applications, can be used to compromise WLAN security implementations. You downloaded a video that demonstrated the use of these tools in identifying cleartext and cracking passwords on a WLAN. This video explained different initialization vectors (IVs) and points of entry into an unprotected or weakly protected WLAN and how to recover an unencrypted WEP key. You also used the information from this lab to craft a WLAN security implementation plan to mitigate any weaknesses and security threats commonly found in a WLAN implementation.

Lab Assessment Questions & Answers

1. What functions do these WLAN applications and tools perform on WLANs: airmon-ng, airodump-ng, and aireplay-ng?

2. Why is it critical to use encryption techniques on a wireless LAN? Which encryption method is best for use on a WLAN (WEP, WPA, WPA2)?

3. What security countermeasures can you enable on your wireless access point (WAP) as part of a layered security solution for WLAN implementations?

4. Why is wireless such an important vector to secure properly for many organizations, including home users?

5. What risks, threats, and vulnerabilities are prominent with WLAN infrastructures?

6. What is the risk of logging onto access points in airports or other public places?

____

____

____

____

7. Why is it important to have a wireless access policy and to conduct regular site surveys and audits?

____

____

____

____

8. What is a risk of using your mobile cell phone or external WLAN as a WiFi connection point?

____

____

____

____

Perform Incident Response for an Infected Microsoft® Windows Workstation

LAB 9

Introduction

This lab is an extension of Lab #6, in which you identified and eliminated malicious software on a Microsoft® Windows workstation. As a member of the Security Incident Response Team, you are assigned a trouble ticket indicating that there are unidentified files on the vWorkstation. In this lab, you will perform a security incident response and forensic analysis on the contaminated workstation. You will be required to document every action taken and its outcome (in text as well as screen captures) in a detailed security incident response report, maintaining a proper chain of custody and recording the date and time for every action performed.

Learning Objectives

Upon completing this lab, you will be able to:

- Use applications and tools to scan a Windows workstation for malicious software and malware
- Identify malicious software and malware that has compromised the workstation
- Isolate and quarantine the Windows workstation for incident response analysis as per chain of custody
- Perform a security incident response on the Windows workstation and document, identify, isolate, and eradicate according to chain of custody
- Draft a security incident response report capturing your date/timestamps, findings, the steps taken, and the solutions for prevention of a recurrence

TOOLS AND SOFTWARE

NAME	MORE INFORMATION
AVG	http://free.avg.com/us-en/homepage
IZarc Archiver	http://www.izarc.org/

Deliverables

Upon completion of this lab, you are required to provide the following deliverables to your instructor:

1. A Security Incident Response Report that includes screen captures and a written description (including date and time) of the actions taken and any outcomes for each incident response phase described in your text: Incident Identification, Triage, Containment, Investigation, Analysis and Tracking, Recovery and Repair, and Debriefing and Feedback;
2. Lab Assessment Questions & Answers for Lab #9.

Hands-On Steps

1. This lab begins with a trouble ticket generated by a nightly system check, as shown here.

   The Security Incident Response Team, of which you are now a member, is responsible for determining what actions to take after receiving notification of a possible incident.

FIGURE 9.1

Trouble ticket received by the Security Incident Response Team

IT Trouble Ticket #001

Category	Malware Found	**Status**	Critical
Title	Unidentified files on the system		
Description	The nightly system check discovered some unidentified files on the vWorkstation.		
Reported by	System log		

2. In a new text document, **create** a **Security Incident Response Report** that includes each of the following headings: Incident Identification, Triage, Containment, Investigation, Analysis and Tracking, Recovery and Repair, and Debriefing and Feedback.

   You will follow the steps in this lab and document your entire process like a forensics investigation as part of chain of custody, including screenshots, date and timestamps, and sentences explaining each action. You will be responsible for determining what to document and which actions fall into the headings established in your text document.

> **Note:**
> The next steps will repeat the steps from Lab #6 to identify and quarantine malware or malicious software, detect a hidden virus embedded in an encrypted file, and eliminate any problems identified by these actions.

3. From the student landing vWorkstation virtual machine desktop, **double-click** the **My Computer icon** on the desktop.
4. **Double-click** the **Local Disk (C:) icon** in the My Computer window.
5. **Double-click** the **Security_Strategies folder.**
6. **Double-click** the **ISSA_TOOLS folder.**
7. **Verify** that the **prodrev.zip file** appears in the folder. This encrypted zip file will be used later in the lab.

FIGURE 9.2

Locating the prodrev.zip file

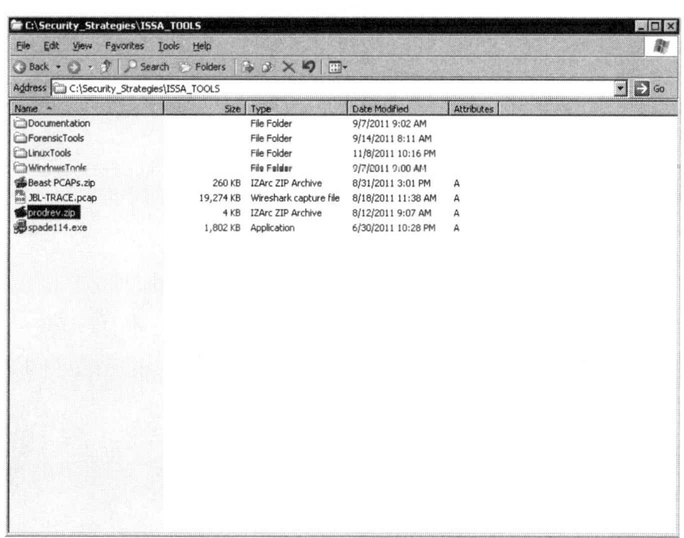

8. **Minimize** the **ISSA_TOOLS folder.**
9. **Double-click** the **AVG 2012 icon** on the desktop to start the antivirus application.
10. **Click** the **Overview button** from the application's navigation bar.

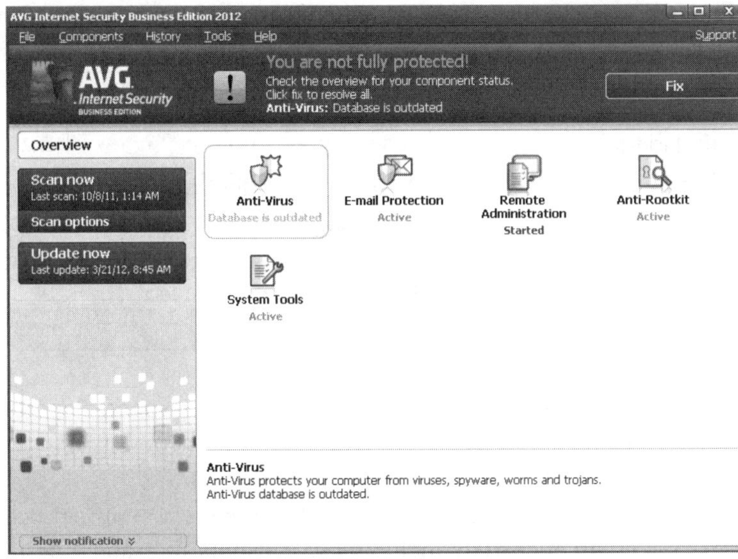

FIGURE 9.3
The AVG 2012 application window

11. **Click** the **Scan now button** in the navigation bar.

    The default scan is a whole computer scan which should be indicated by a green arrow beneath the Scan option button in the navigation bar. This scan will take several minutes. Do not touch any keys until the scan is finished.

    When the scan is completed, AVG will display a summary of the threats that it identified and removed.

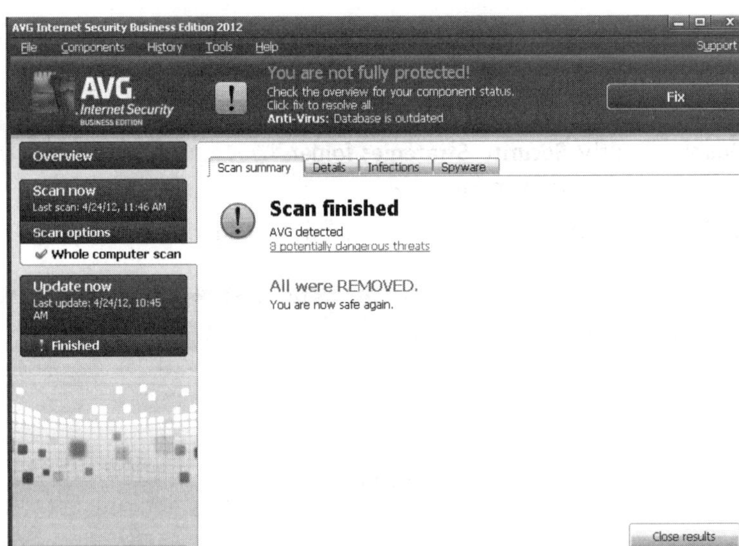

FIGURE 9.4
Scan summary for completed scan

12. In a new text document, **record** the **number of threats** identified by the scan.

13. **Click** the **Details tab** to see more specifics about the types of threats AVG identified.

FIGURE 9.5

Detailed summary of identified threats

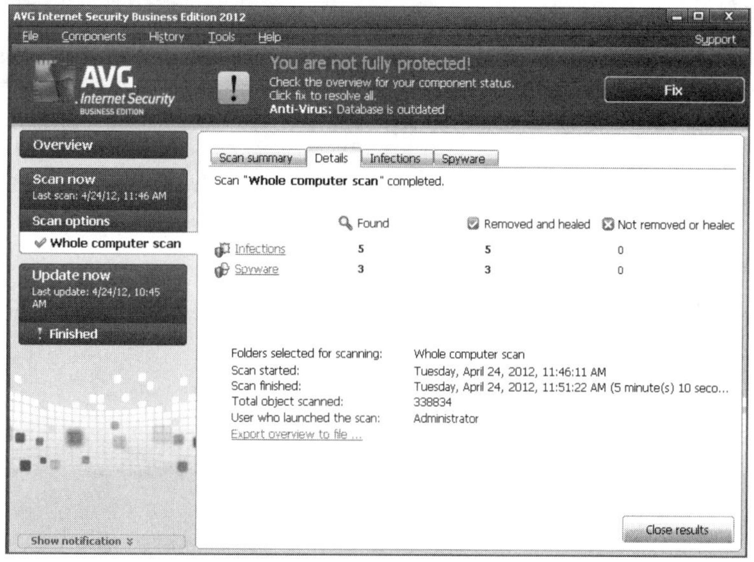

14. **Click** the **Infections tab** to see the specific infections found in this scan.

FIGURE 9.6

Infections identified in this scan

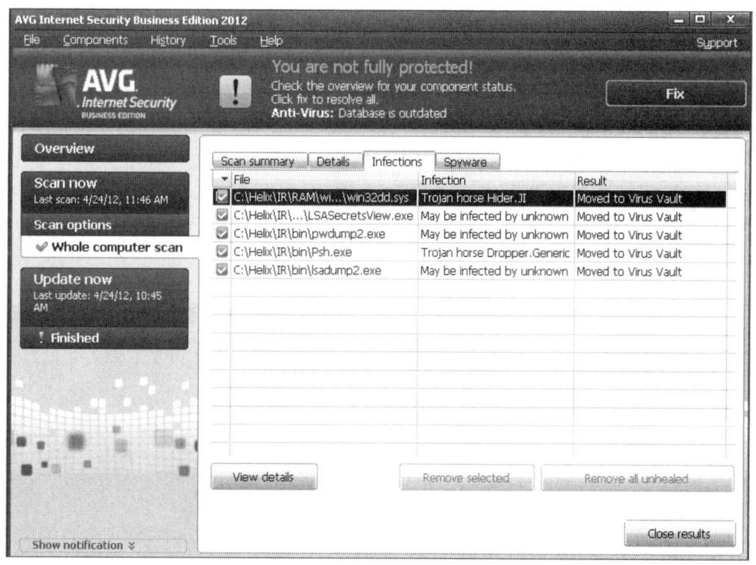

15. **Click** the first identified **infection**, and then **click** the **View details button** at the bottom of the window to get more information about it.
16. From a workstation with an Internet connection, **research** the **infection** found on this screen and the possible remediation steps. **Document your findings** in your text document.
17. **Click** the **Close button** to return to the Infections tab.
18. **Repeat** steps 15 through 17 for each of the threats identified by AVG.

19. **Click** the **Spyware tab** to see the specific spyware found in this scan.

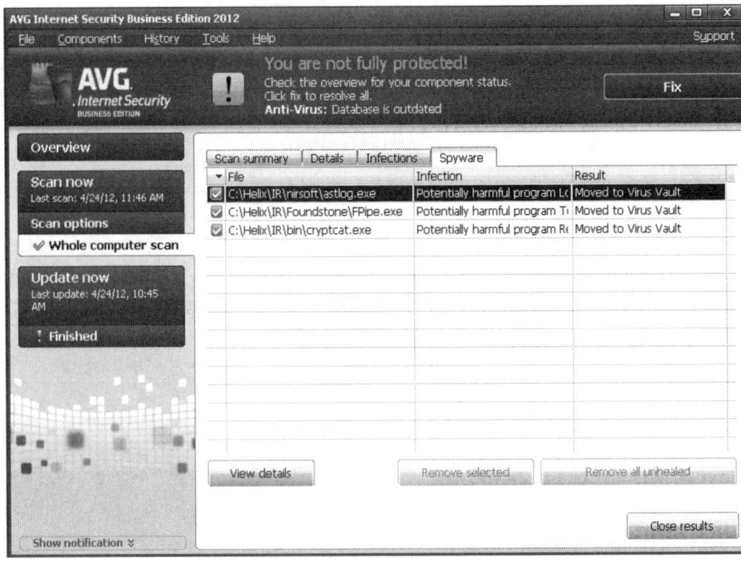

FIGURE 9.7

Spyware and other malicious software identified in this scan

20. **Click** the first identified **spyware**, and then **click** the **View details button** at the bottom of the window to get more information about it.
21. From a workstation with an Internet connection, **research** the **spyware** found on this screen and the possible remediation steps. **Document your findings** in your text document.
22. **Click** the **Close button** to return to the Spyware tab.
23. **Repeat** steps 20 through 22 for each of the threats identified by AVG.
24. **Select History > Virus Vault** from the AVG menu to confirm that all malicious software and malware identified by the scan is properly quarantined.

    Notice that the tool did not identify the prodrev.zip file because antivirus software cannot open encrypted files for scanning.

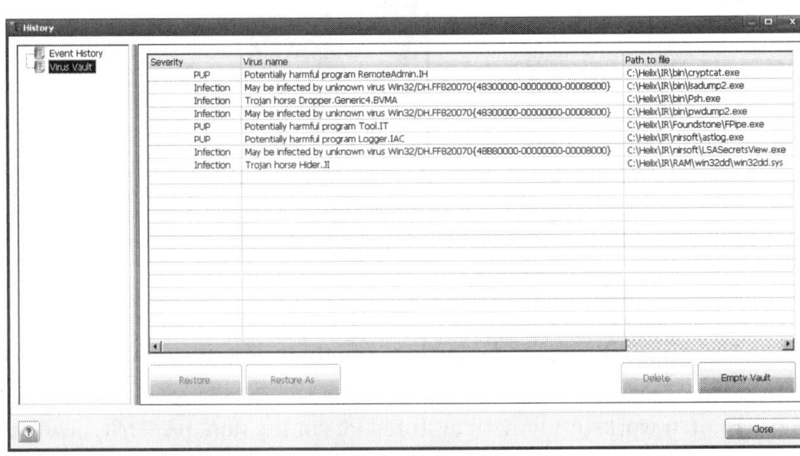

FIGURE 9.8

AVG's Virus Vault

25. **Click** the **Empty Vault button** to delete any virus, malware, and malicious software detected by the application.
26. **Click Yes** to confirm the process.
27. **Click Close** to close the Virus Vault.

28. **Maximize** the **ISSA_TOOLS folder.**
29. **Right-click** the **prodrev.zip file.**
30. **Click IZarc** and **Extract Here** from the context menu.

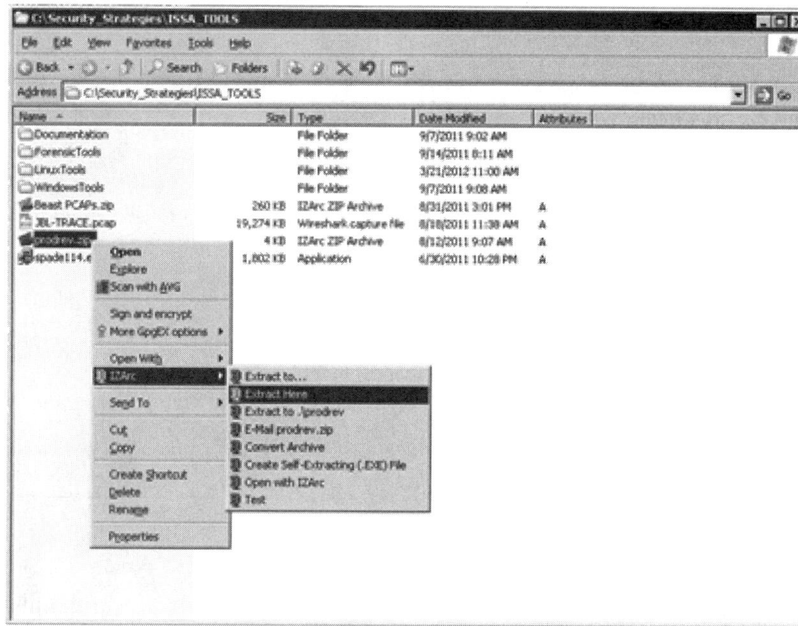

FIGURE 9.9

Extracting the encrypted file

31. When prompted, **type password123** (the document's password) in the password dialog box.
    The newly extracted file, productreview.pdf, will appear in the ISSA_TOOLS folder.
32. **Double-click** the **productreview.pdf file** and **type password123** (the document's password) in the password dialog box to open the file.
    AVG, still running in the background, will detect the virus within the file and display an alert message.

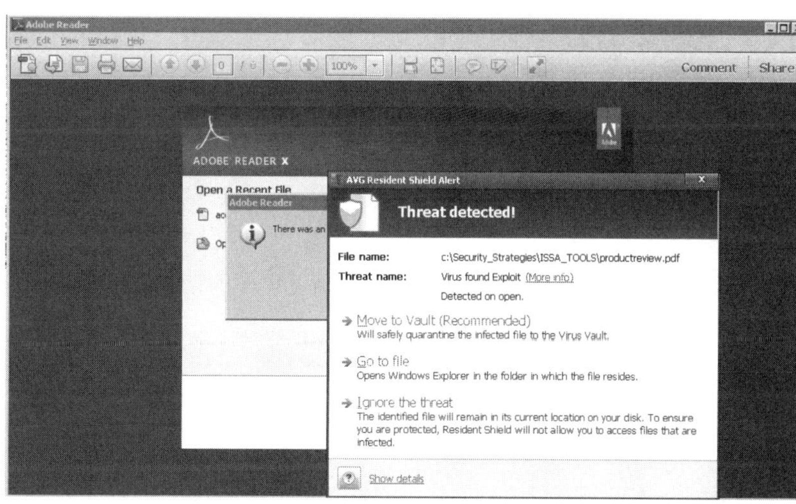

FIGURE 9.10

AVG's Threat Detected alert

33. **Click** the **Move to Vault (Recommended)** option to quarantine the file within AVG's vault.
34. **Click Close** to close the alert message.
35. **Click OK** to close the Adobe error message and **close Adobe Reader**.

36. **Close** the **ISSA_TOOLS folder** to bring the AVG software to the forefront.
37. In the AVG toolbar, **click History** and **select Virus Vault**.
38. If necessary, **expand** the **Path to file column width** as necessary to **verify** that the **productreview.pdf file** is displayed in the vault.

FIGURE 9.11

The AVG Virus Vault

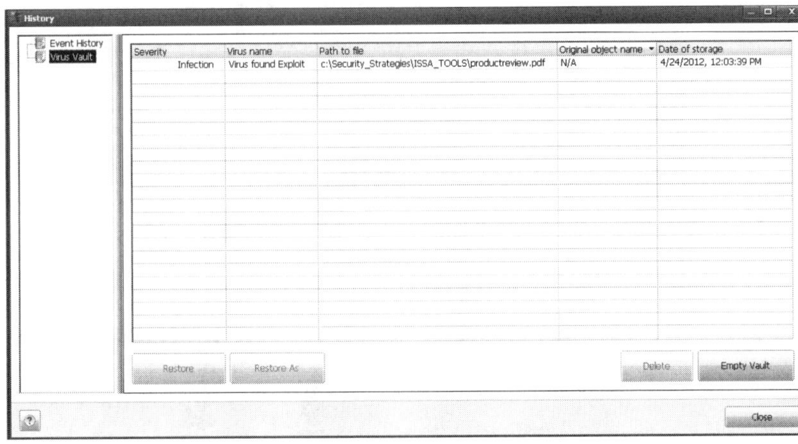

39. **Click** the **Empty Vault button** to delete any virus, malware, and malicious software detected by the application.
40. **Click Yes** to confirm the process.
41. **Click Close** to close the Virus Vault.
42. **Close** the **AVG window**.
43. **Review** your **text document** to make sure that you have included all of the elements necessary for a proper security incident response report.
44. Use the **File Transfer button** to download the **text file** to your local computer and submit it as part of your deliverables.

Evaluation Criteria and Rubrics

The following are the evaluation criteria and rubrics for Lab #9 that students must perform:

1. Was the student able to use applications and tools to scan a Windows workstation for malicious software and malware? – [**20%**]
2. Was the student able to identify malicious software and malware that has compromised the workstation? – [**20%**]
3. Was the student able to isolate and quarantine the Windows workstation for incident response analysis as per chain of custody? – [**20%**]
4. Was the student able to perform a security incident response on the Windows workstation and document, identify, isolate, and eradicate according to chain of custody? – [**20%**]
5. Was the student able to draft a security incident response report capturing date/timestamps, findings, the steps taken, and the solutions for prevention of a recurrence? – [**20%**]

LAB #9 – ASSESSMENT WORKSHEET

Perform Incident Response for an Infected Microsoft® Windows Workstation

Course Name and Number: _______________

Student Name: _______________

Instructor Name: _______________

Lab Due Date: _______________

Overview

This lab is an extension of a previous lab in which you identified and eliminated malicious software on a Microsoft® Windows workstation. As a member of the Security Incident Response Team, you were assigned a trouble ticket indicating that there were unidentified files on the vWorkstation. In this lab, you performed a security incident response and forensic analysis on the contaminated workstation. You documented every action taken and its outcome (in text as well as screen captures) in a detailed security incident response report, maintaining proper chain of custody and recording the date and times for every action performed.

Lab Assessment Questions & Answers

1. When you are notified that a user's workstation or system is acting strangely and log files indicate system compromise, what is the first thing you should do to the workstation or system and why?

____

____

____

____

2. When an antivirus application identifies a virus and quarantines this file, does this mean the computer is free of the virus and any malicious software?

____

____

____

____

3. Where would you check for processes and services enabled in the background of your "Student" vWorkstation?

4. Where would log files typically be kept on most Microsoft® systems?

5. What is the SANS Institute's six-step incident handling process?

6. What is the risk of containing an incident prior to completing the identification process?

7. Why would an organization want to have the incident response handled by the security incident response team and not the IT organization?

8. Do you think it is a good idea to have a security policy that defines the incident response process in your organization? Why or why not?

9. Do you think it is a good idea to have internal legal counsel notified when a "Critical" security incident occurs?

____

____

____

____

10. What is the last step in the incident handling process, and what is its importance?

____

____

____

____

Design and Implement SNORT as an Intrusion Detection System (IDS)

LAB 10

Introduction

In this lab, you will configure SNORT as an intrusion detection system (IDS) on the BackTrack4 virtual machine and configure the IDS monitoring tool called BASE. You also will use the Nessus® scanning tool to scan the BackTrack4 virtual machine to test the SNORT configuration and see exactly what circumstances trigger an IDS alert. Nessus requires a high screen resolution. If your resolution is below 1024x768, some information may not fit on the screen. Check your screen resolution now to proceed through the lab without interruption.

Learning Objectives

Upon completing this lab, you will be able to:

- Set up and configure a SNORT intrusion detection system (IDS) to properly run, detect, and alert in the event of a network-based attack
- Configure BASE, an IDS alert monitoring tool, to view alerting events on a running IDS system
- Recognize IDS signatures, rules, and other IDS components
- Use scanning tools to scan the IDS system with attacks that will alert and understand how the output of scans appears as events in an IDS
- Document and describe the attacks detected to be able to tell whether they are false positives or if there is a need to remediate a vulnerability

TOOLS AND SOFTWARE

NAME	MORE INFORMATION
BackTrack	http://www.backtrack-linux.org/
MySQL	http://www.mysql.com
Basic Analysis and Security Engine (BASE)	http://base.secureideas.net/

Deliverables

Upon completion of this lab, you are required to provide the following deliverables to your instructor:

1. A text document that includes each of the following items:
    a. A screen capture of the host detail screen from the Lab #10 SNORT Scan;
    b. A screen capture of the BASE alerts detail screen;
    c. A screen capture of an individual BASE alert detail;
    d. A screen capture of an ATTACK RESPONSE on the BASE alert detail screen;
2. Lab Assessment Questions & Answers for Lab #10.

Hands-On Steps

1. This lab begins at the student landing vWorkstation virtual machine desktop of the VSCL, as shown here.

FIGURE 10.1
"Student Landing" VSCL workstation

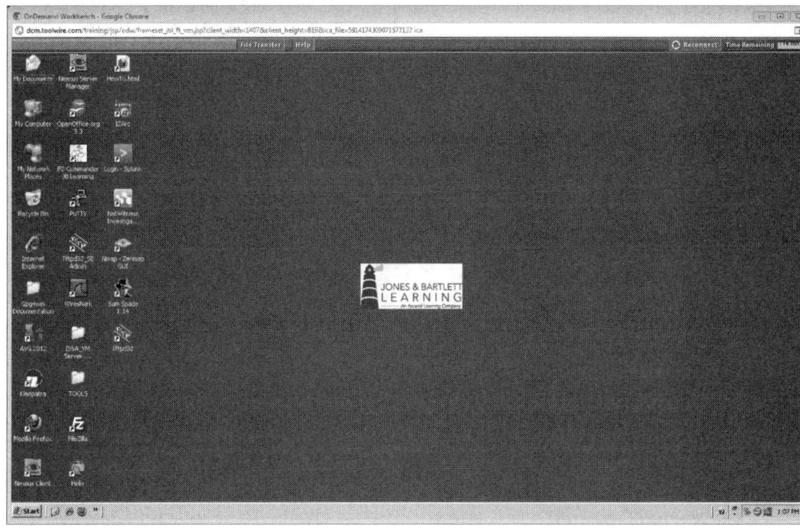

> **Note:**
> The next steps will configure SNORT as an intrusion detection system (IDS) on the BackTrack4 virtual machine to detect a Nessus® vulnerability scan.

2. **Double-click** the **ISSA_VM Server Farm_RDP icon** on the desktop.
3. **Double-click** the **BackTrack4 icon** to open that application.

FIGURE 10.2
Open a remote connection to the BackTrack4 virtual machine

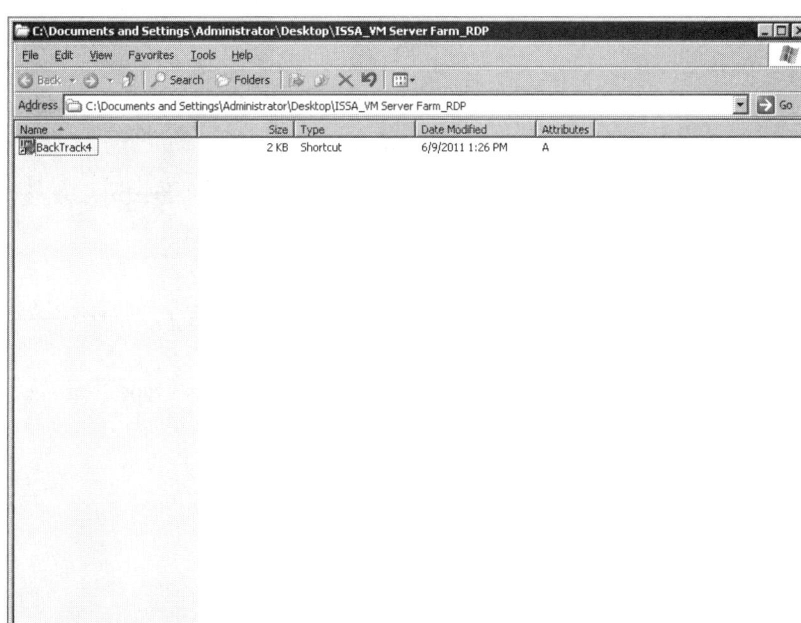

4. **Log in** to the **BackTrack4 Framework** using the following security credentials:
    - Login: **root**
    - Password: **toor**

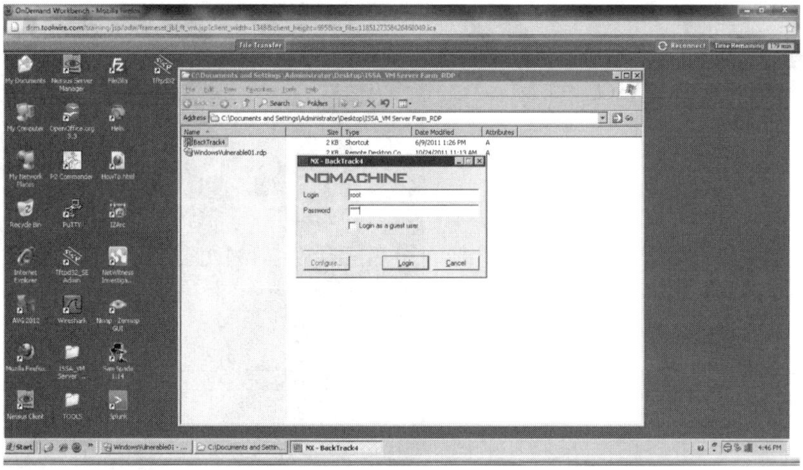

FIGURE 10.3
BackTrack4 login screen

5. **Click** the **K menu icon** in the toolbar at the bottom of the window and **select Services > SNORT > Setup and Initialize SNORT**.

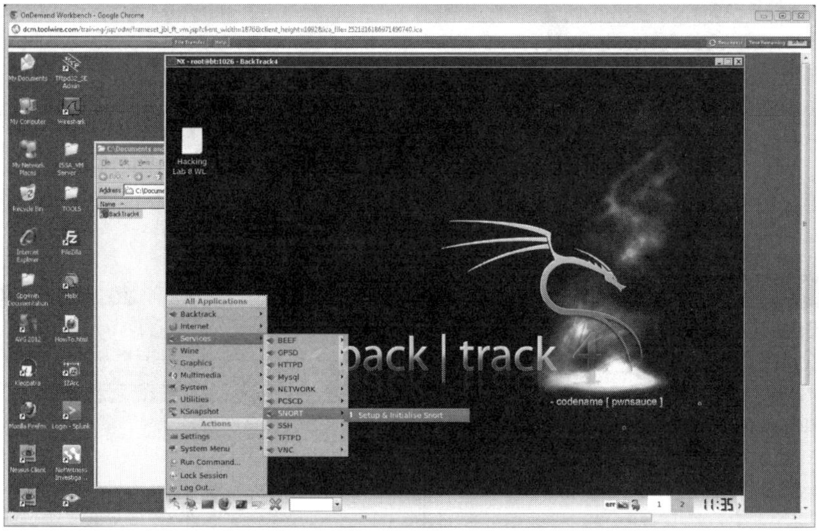

FIGURE 10.4
Opening the SNORT application

6. When prompted for a MySQL root password, **type toor**.
7. When prompted for a MySQL SNORT user password, **type toor**.

8. When prompted to install SNORT, MySQL, and Apache/BASE, **type Y** and **press Enter**.

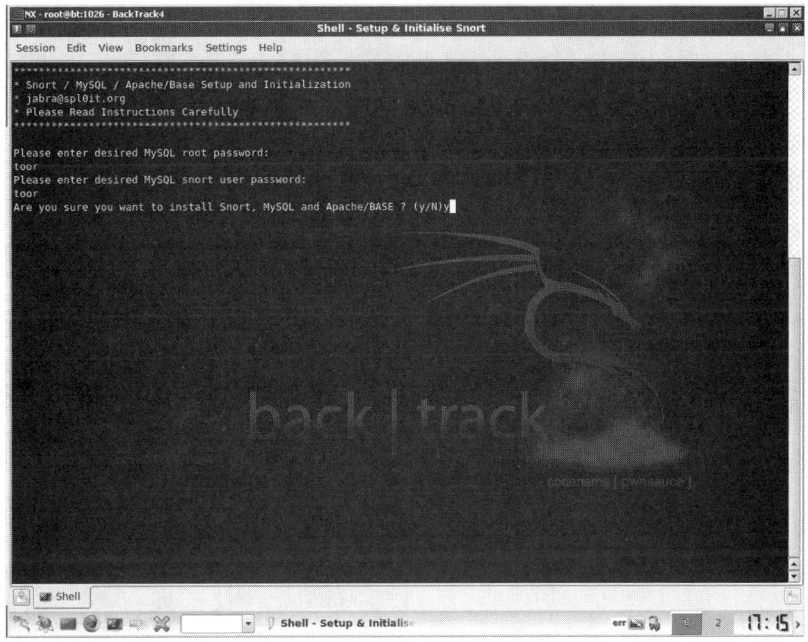

FIGURE 10.5
Installing SNORT

9. The initialization process is completed when the terminal prompt (root@bt:#) appears. SNORT is now running and is configured with the default alerts and rules (signatures). **Document** the **IP address** for the BASE Frontend to Snort which can be found above the terminal prompt: (*BaseIP:=* ________________ ________________________). You will use this address in a later step.

   Remember that IP addresses are formatted in a dotted decimal notation that divides the address into four groups of numbers representing 8 bits apiece.

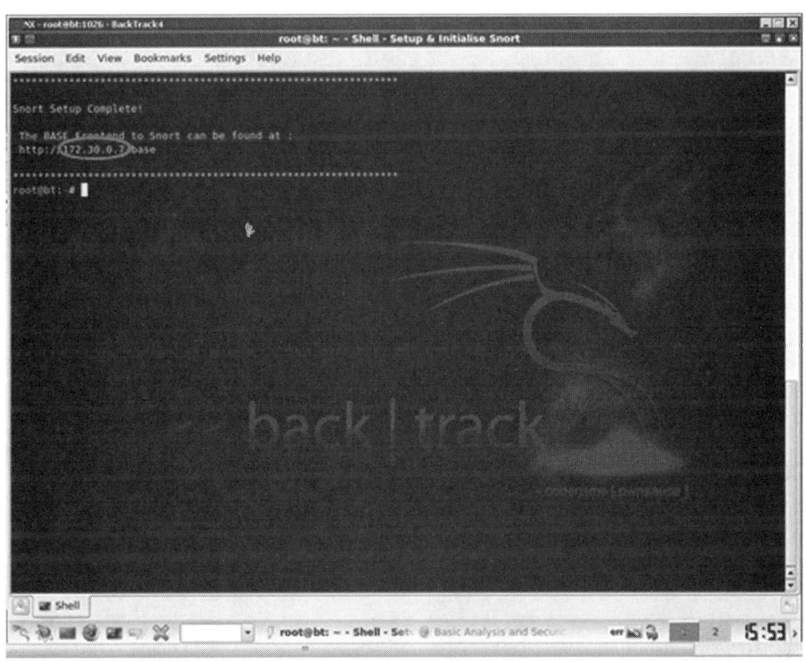

FIGURE 10.6
Identifying the *BaseIP*

Note:
The next steps will use the Basic Analysis and Security Engine (BASE) tool to review traffic statistics on the BackTrack4 virtual machine. BASE is a Web-based tool that analyzes intrusions detected by SNORT.

10. **Double-click** the **Firefox Web Browser icon** in the toolbar at the bottom of the BackTrack4 window.

FIGURE 10.7

Starting the Firefox Web browser

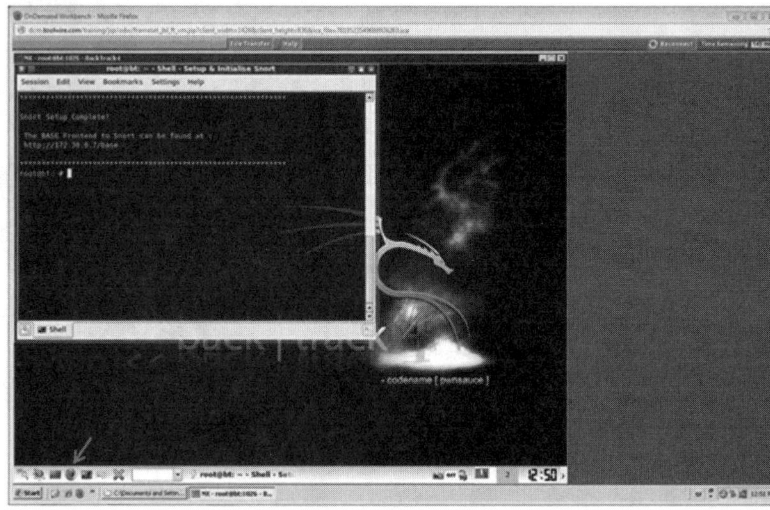

11. In the browser's address bar, **type http://*BaseIP*/base** (using the *BaseIP* address you documented in step 9) to open the BASE alert screen.

    Items in bold or in blue text are links that will open to further detail. Explore the links on this page to familiarize yourself with the features of BASE.

FIGURE 10.8

The BASE alert screen

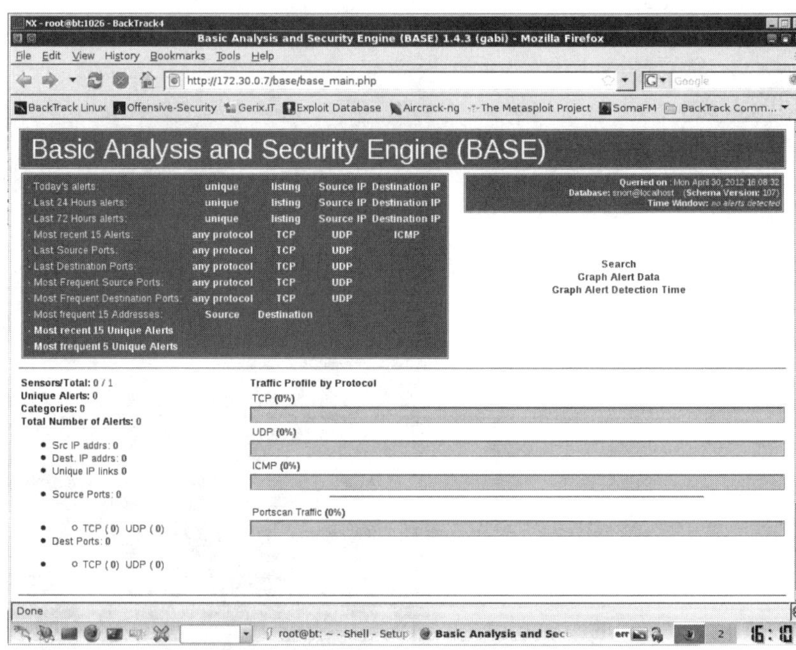

Note:
The next steps will use Nessus® to perform a vulnerability scan on the BackTrack4 virtual machine. First, you will create a new user account with administrative privileges, then create a new policy definition, and run the scan.

12. **Minimize** the **BackTrack4 window** to return to the vWorkstation desktop.

> **Note:**
> The next steps will use Nessus® to perform a vulnerability scan on the BackTrack4 virtual machine. First, you will create a new user account with administrative privileges, then create a new policy definition, and run the scan. As you read in the introduction to the lab, Nessus requires a high screen resolution. If your resolution is below 1024x768, some information may not fit on the screen.
>
> If your resolution is set lower than the recommended setting and you are unable to increase it, then remove some of the browser toolbars as a workaround. In Firefox on the remote desktop, click **View > Toolbars** and **remove (uncheck)** the **Status Bar** and **Bookmarks Bar**. If you are still unable to see the complete application, you can also uncheck the Address Bar.
>
> If you uncheck the Menu Bar you will no longer be able to see the View button to add and remove bars. You can also click and drag the Taskbar from the bottom of the screen to the side of the screen for additional room.

13. From the vWorkstation desk, **double-click** the **Nessus Server Manager icon** to launch the application. The Nessus Server Manager will indicate that the service is running. If the service is stopped, **click** the **Start Nessus Server button** to restart the service.

FIGURE 10.9
Connecting to Nessus®

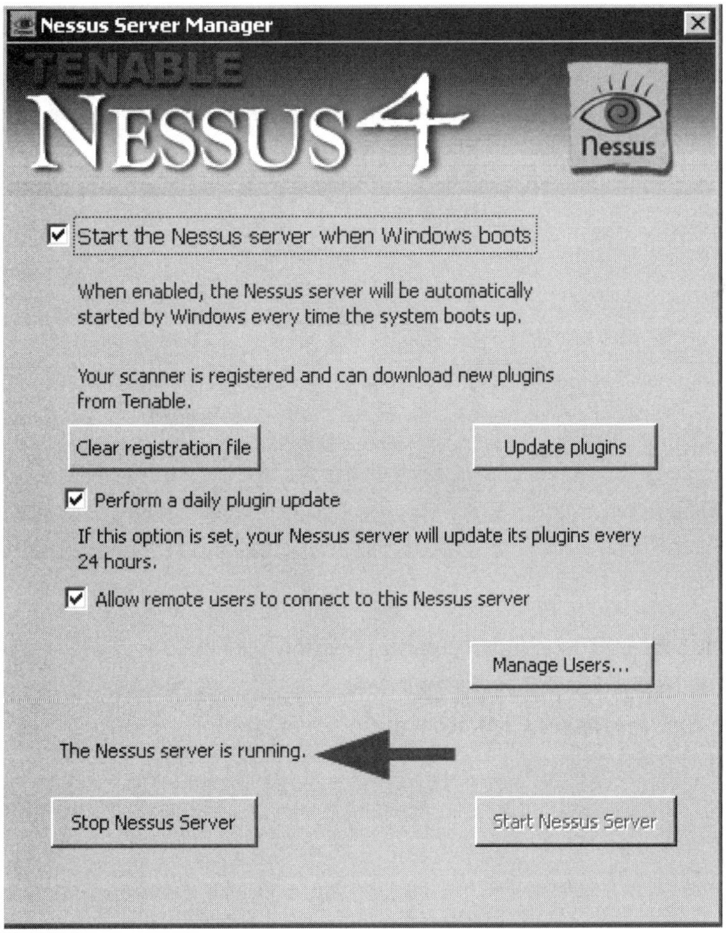

14. **Click** the **Manage Users button** on the Nessus Server Manager window to add a new user account.
15. In the Nessus User Management dialog box, **click** on the **+ button** in the bottom left corner to open the **Add/Edit a user** dialog box.

16. **Type** the following login information:
    - User name: **student**
    - Password: **ISS316Security**
    - Password (again): **ISS316Security**
17. **Select** the **Administrator checkbox** to give this user administrative privileges.

FIGURE 10.10

Add/Edit a user in Nessus Server Manager

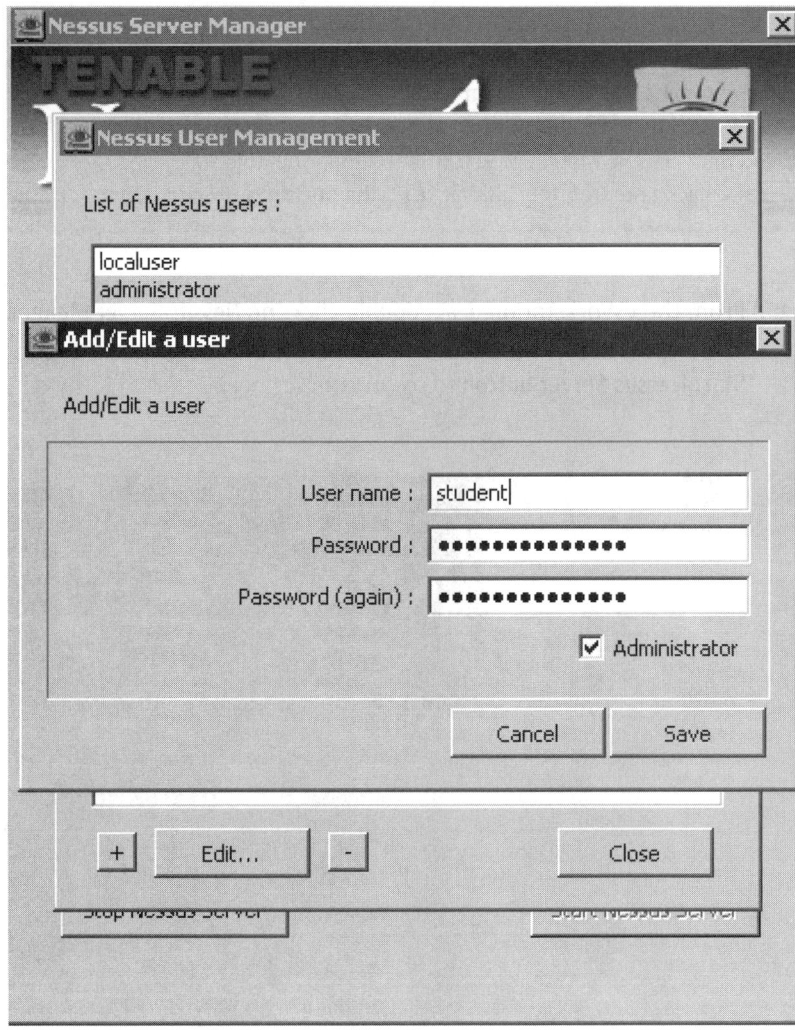

18. **Click** the **Save** button to finish creating the new user account, and then **click Close**.
19. **Close** the **Nessus Server Manager window**.
20. **Double-click** the **Nessus Client icon** on the vWorkstation desktop to open the application in Internet Explorer browser.

Note:

The first time you connect to the Nessus Client, you will see a Web page that tells you that *There is a problem with this website's security certificate*. To proceed any further, you must click the Continue to this website (not recommended) link.

FIGURE 10.11

Certificate problem warning message

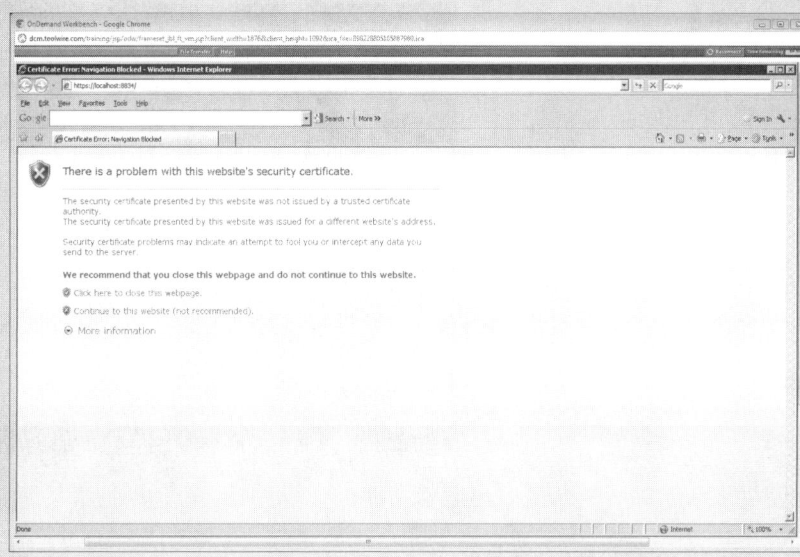

21. When the Nessus Client site appears, log in using the new user account you created in step 15:
    - User name: **student**
    - Password: **ISS316Security**

FIGURE 10.12

Log in to Nessus®

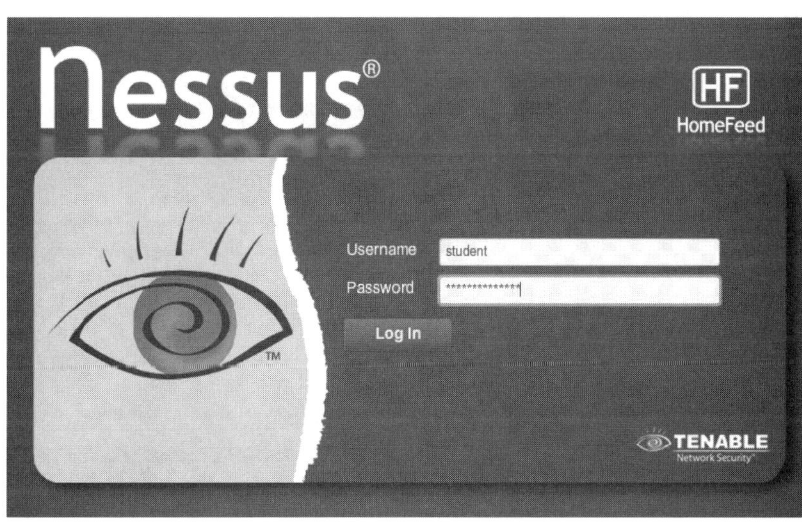

22. **Click** the **Log In button**.
23. **Click OK** to accept the Nessus HomeFeed Terms of Use and open the Nessus Client homepage.
24. **Click** the **Policies tab** on the Nessus Client homepage.

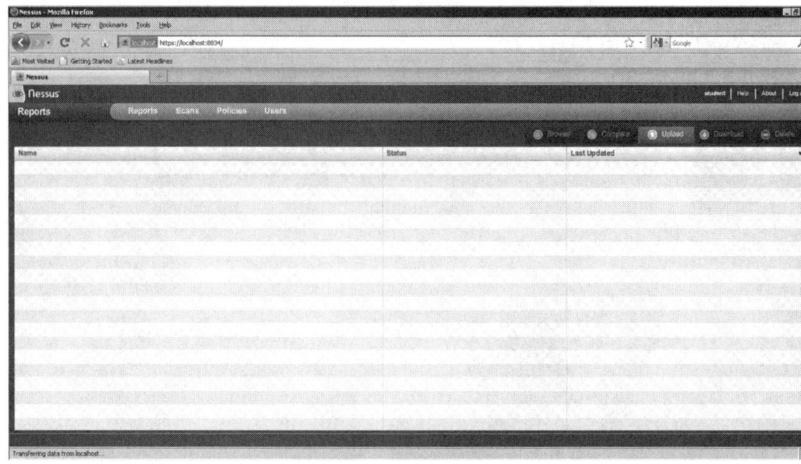

FIGURE 10.13

Nessus Client homepage

25. **Click** the **Add button** to add a new policy.
26. In the **Name** box, **type Lab #10 SNORT Policy** and **click Next twice**.
27. In the Plugins tab, **click** the **Enable All button** and **click Next** to open the Preferences tab.
28. Save the **Lab #10 SNORT Policy** parameters by clicking **Submit** on the final screen.

    The newly created Lab #10 SNORT Policy now appears on the Policies page.

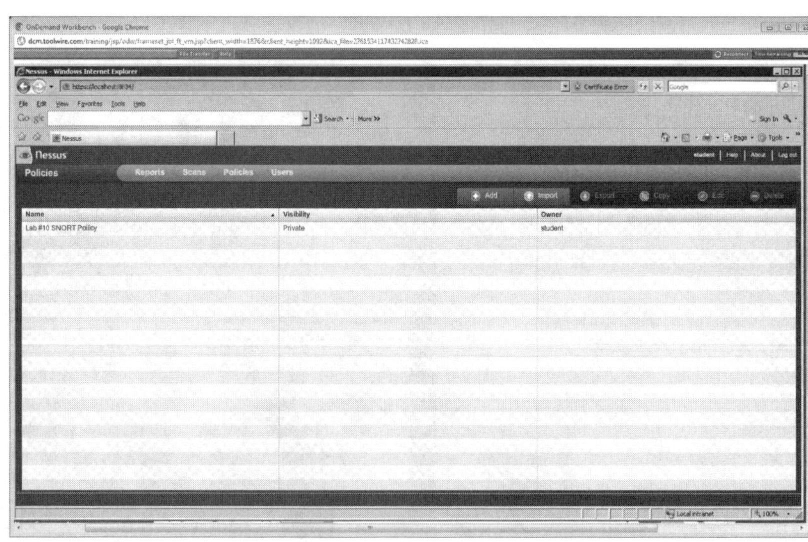

FIGURE 10.14

Selecting Plugins for the Lab #10 SNORT Policy

29. **Click** the **Scans tab** on the Nessus Client toolbar.
30. **Click** the **Add button** to add a new scan and use the information in the following steps to configure the scan.
31. In the **Name** box, **type Lab #10 SNORT Scan**.
32. In the **Type** box, **select Run Now** from the drop-down menu.
33. In the **Policy** box, **select Lab #10 SNORT Policy** from the drop-down menu.
34. In the **Scan Targets** box, **type *BaseIP*/24** (using the *BaseIP* address you documented in step 9).
35. Leave the **Targets File** box empty.

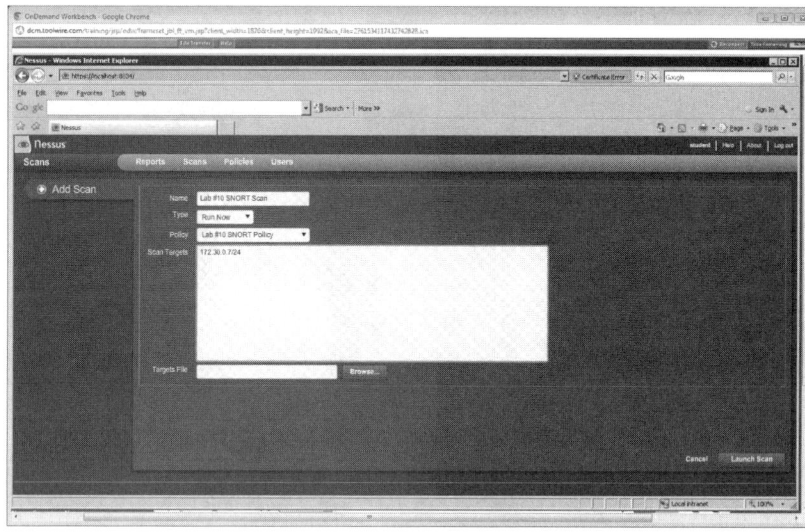

FIGURE 10.15

Creating parameters for Lab #10 SNORT Scan

36. **Click** the **Launch Scan button** to start the scan.

    The scan will begin immediately and a status bar, colored yellow, will indicate the progress of the scan. You can use the control buttons at the top of the Scans screen to Pause, Resume, or Stop the scan. Use the Browse button to see more detail about the progress of the scan for each target being scanned.

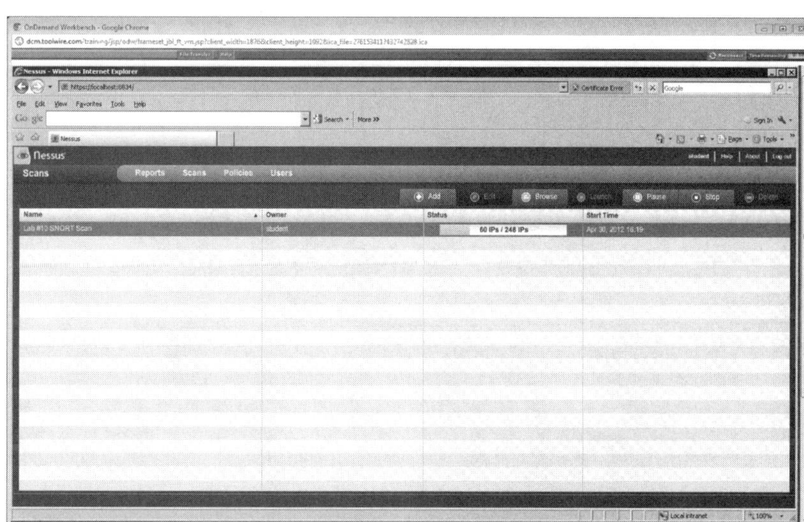

FIGURE 10.16

Lab #10 SNORT Scan progress bar

37. **Click** the **Reports tab** in the toolbar at the top to show the running and completed scans. The Reports screen acts as a central point for viewing, comparing, uploading, and downloading scan results.
38. **Double-click** the **Lab #10 SNORT Scan** line item to open the report for that scan.

    The first screen you see is the summary screen, which gives an overview of hosts scanned and vulnerabilities discovered. Vulnerabilities are categorized according to severity: High, Medium, and Low. You can also access the scan report by first clicking on the report name and then clicking the Browse button.

FIGURE 10.17
Nessus® report summary

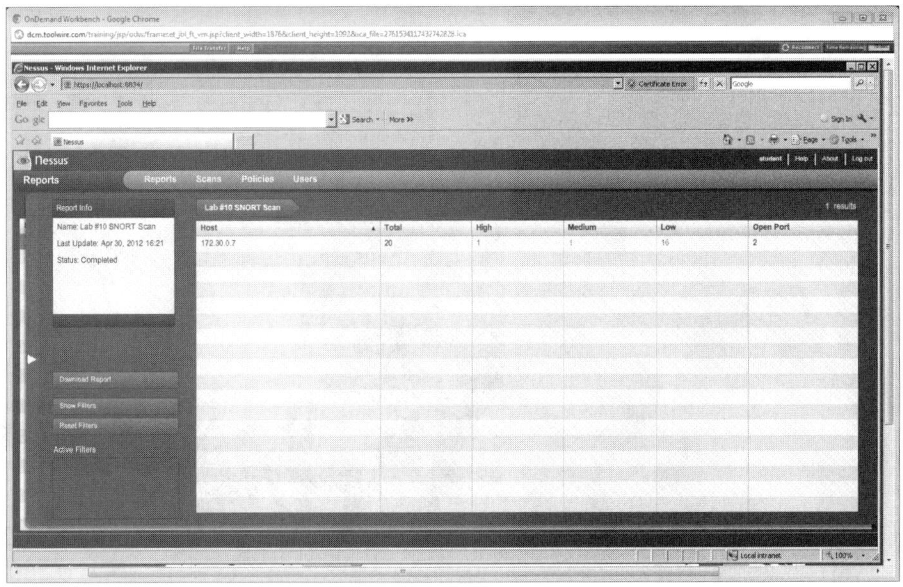

39. **Double-click** the **Host URL** to review the items found by this scan.
40. **Make a screen capture** of the host detail screen and **paste** it into a new text document.

> **Note:**
> To capture the screen, press the **Ctrl** and **PrtSc** keys together, and then **use Ctrl + V** to paste the image into a Word or other word processor document.

41. **Close** the **Internet Explorer browser window** to exit from the Nessus Client.

42. **Close** the **Nessus Server Manager** to bring the BASE alert screen to the front.

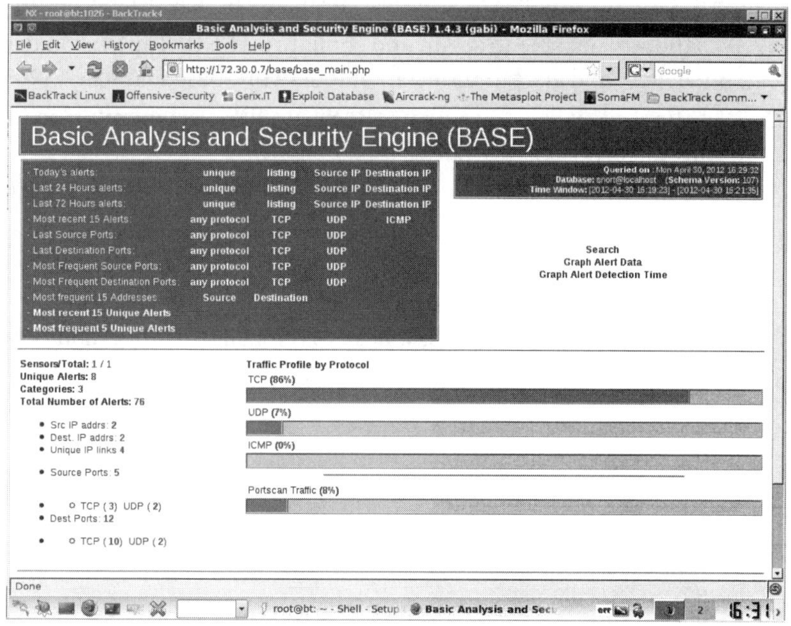

FIGURE 10.18
BASE alert screen showing SNORT alerts

43. **Make a screen capture** of the BASE alert screen showing alerts identified by SNORT and **paste** it into your text document.
44. **Click** the **Total Number of Alerts link** at the left of the screen to open the alerts detail screen.
45. **Make a screen capture** of the alerts detail screen and **paste** it into your text document. You may have to take multiple screen captures to display the entire output.
46. **Review** the **various links** on this page to see the alerts that the BASE analysis tool has captured and organized.
47. **Locate** one of the ATTACK-RESPONSES 403 Forbidden errors in the Signatures column and then **click** the **corresponding link in the ID column** to open the detail page.
48. **Make a screen capture** of the details screen and **paste** it into your text document. You may have to take multiple screen captures to display the entire output.
49. **Close** the **BackTrack4 window**.
50. **Click Disconnect** when prompted to disconnect the session and return to the vWorkstation desktop.
51. Use the **File Transfer button** to download the **text file** to your local computer and submit it as part of your deliverables.

Evaluation Criteria and Rubrics

The following are the evaluation criteria and rubrics for Lab #10 that the students must perform:

1. Was the student able to set up and configure a SNORT intrusion detection system (IDS) to properly run, detect, and alert in the event of a network-based attack? – [**20%**]
2. Was the student able to configure BASE, an IDS alert monitoring tool, to view alerting events on a running IDS system? – [**20%**]
3. Was the student able to recognize IDS signatures, rules, and other IDS components? – [**20%**]
4. Was the student able to use scanning tools to scan the IDS system with attacks that will alert and understand how the output of scans appears as events in an IDS? – [**20%**]
5. Was the student able to document and describe the attacks detected to be able to identify whether they are false positives or if there is a need to remediate a vulnerability? – [**20%**]

LAB #10 – ASSESSMENT WORKSHEET

Design and Implement SNORT as an Intrusion Detection System (IDS)

Course Name and Number: _______________

Student Name: _______________

Instructor Name: _______________

Lab Due Date: _______________

Overview

In this lab, you configured SNORT as an intrusion detection system (IDS) on the BackTrack4 virtual machine and configured the IDS monitoring tool called BASE. You also used the Nessus® scanning tool to scan the BackTrack4 virtual machine to test the SNORT configuration and see exactly what circumstances trigger an IDS alert.

Lab Assessment Questions & Answers

1. What is the difference between an intrusion detection system (IDS) or an intrusion prevention system (IPS)?

2. Why is it important to perform a network traffic baseline definition analysis?

3. As the network security administrator, why would you be alarmed to detect a Nessus® port scan from an internal IP address?

4. Are the packets that SNORT IDS captures off the LAN segment for examination saved or logged?

5. What is the difference between host-based IDS and network-based IDS systems?

6. How can you prevent attackers performing reconnaissance and probing, with Nmap and Nessus® port scanning and vulnerability assessment scanning tools?

7. Why is it a good idea to have host-based IDS enabled on critical servers and workstations?

8. Where should you implement IPS in your IT infrastructure?